THE TRAIL OF MANY
SPIRITS
PAWS • WINGS • HOOVES • MOCCASINS

WRITTEN AND PHOTOGRAPHED
By
SERLE CHAPMAN

CHIEF JOSEPH

LITTLE CROW

GERONIMO

SITTING BULL

BRITISH COLUMBIA

ALBERTA

SASKATCHEWAN

MANITOBA

MONTANA

NORTH DAKOTA

MINNESOTA

SOUTH DAKOTA

IDAHO

WYOMING

ROCKY MTS

NEBRASKA

IOWA

UTAH

COLORADO

MISSOURI

KANSAS

ARIZONA

NEW MEXICO

OKLAHOMA

ARKANSAS

TEXAS

CALGARY

REGINA

WINNIPEG

GLACIER N.P.

MILK R.

KALISPELL

YELLOW STONE R.

KNIFE RIVER

BISMARCK

FT. LINCOLN

MILLE LACS

LOLO

MISSOULA

POWDER RIVER

MPLS ST PAUL

FT SNELLING

CLEAR WATER R.

BITTER ROOT

BOZEMAN

BIG HORN R.

MISSOURI RIVER

MISSISSIPPI RIVER

KAMIAH

ROSE BUD R.

BELLE FOURCHE R.

IDAHO

SAWTOOTH MTS

CODY

SHERIDAN

BEAR BUTTE

PIERRE

FLANDREAU

PIPESTONE

BOISE

YELLOWSTONE N.P.

BIG HORN MTS

BLACK HILLS

R. CITY

BAD LANDS

SIOUX FALLS

DESMOINES RIVER

JACKSON

PINE RIDGE

SIOUX CITY

CASPER

FT. ROBINSON

OMAHA

DESMOINES

GREAT SALT LAKE

FT. LARAMIE

N. PLATTE R.

PLATTE RIVER

SALT LAKE C.

CHEYENNE

JULES BURG

ARCHES NP

S. PLATTE R.

KANSAS CITY

CANYON LANDS NP

MOAB

GRAND JUNCTION

GUNNISON

DENVER

BRYCE CANYON NP

COLORADO RIVER

ARKANSAS RIVER

WICHITA

COLORADO SPRINGS

MESA VERDE

CANYON DE CHELLY

GRAND CANYON NP

PAINTED DESERT

SANTA FE

OKLAHOMA CITY

PHOENIX

ALBUQUERQUE

RED RIVER

TALAROSA MTS

SAGUARO N.M.

TUCSON

ELK MTS

FT. WORTH

DALLAS

TOMB STONE

SAN ANTONIO

HOUSTON

TILLETT

THE TRAIL OF MANY
SPIRITS

IN A LITTLE OVER
TWENTY YEARS
six

FOREWORD
BY SONNY SKYHAWK
seven

GO WEST
YOUNG MAN . . .
nine

WEST, ACROSS THE
MISSISSIPPI
fifteen

BEYOND THE
POWDER RIVER
C O U N T R Y
twenty-nine

ON THE TRAIL OF THE
RIO GRANDE
forty-seven

I knew the name of Sitting Bull before that of Winston Churchill. I knew who he was, I knew his nation and I knew some of the history, but not the irony, of the adversary to whom he would forever be bound. In my imagination Ilkley Moor became the 'Wild West', and as a boy I scrambled through the blanket of ferns that spring and summer cast across the peat and heather to launch ambush after ambush, all before tea-time. It didn't matter what tribe I was, only that I was an 'Indian' and the unsuspecting hikers were 'Cowboys'. At home my mother would gently remind me that 'brung' and other such words and phrases from the scripts of Hollywood westerns 'were improper English'. Then my sister would explain why the movies I watched so avidly weren't truthful, a reality I was thankful for because in my heart I never wanted the cavalry to arrive.

It took me a little over twenty years to span the divide that existed between the lure of those childhood dreams and actually crossing the Great Plains of the American West with a latter-day pony from a stable of 'Rent-a-Cars', and American Airlines' wings of the air. When some still called the West wild, a comparative period of time saw the continent braced by the first of four transcontinental railways. Only sixteen years elapsed between the then Secretary of War, Jefferson Davis, ordering the Topographical Corps to survey the West for a feasible rail route, and May 1869 when, at Promontory Point, Utah, Samuel Montague and Grenville M. Dodge of the Central and Union Pacific Railroads respectively, shook hands beside the spike that united them.

The Pony Express lived and died in nine months, and with the railroad came telegraph wires, tent towns, saloons and gold-diggers of every kind. The likes of William F. 'Buffalo Bill' Cody, a redundant Pony Express rider, contributed to the wanton slaughter of the buffalo – in three years eight million were butchered for their hides. So efficient were these buffalo hunters of European extraction that, by the mid-1880s, only three hundred bison out of an estimated seventy-five million survived on the American Plains. It took less than twenty years for Crazy Horse and Custer to become both heroes, and martyrs, in their people's eyes. In one afternoon the population of Guthrie, Oklahoma, went from zero to ten thousand and, at the OK Corral in Tombstone, Arizona, Wyatt Earp became a legend in twenty-seven seconds. What had begun with Columbus, continued with Francisco Vásquez de Coronado, moored with the *Mayflower* and accelerated with Lewis and Clark on Thomas Jefferson's 'Voyage of Discovery', *appeared* to be over. In a little over twenty years much of the West had been won, or lost. But the struggle had only just begun.

I first travelled Westward to research a novel I had long felt compelled to write, and amid the inspiration and isolation I discovered all that I'd yearned for and why it consumed me. For as long as my memory allowed, right up to the first minute I spent alone on the prairie, I'd sought the meaning and reason. Then, as I felt that circle close in the arms of whatever time might be, I found myself within it, born wild, or what others might describe as free.

IN A LITTLE OVER TWENTY YEARS
PREFACE

I am still writing that novel. A combination of luck, friendships and belief gave this book life. I borrowed a camera from my brother 'just in case', but initially photography was not my intention – I'm a trier, not a photographer. In the text, I have primarily used the familiar titles associated with Native American Nations but, where possible, I have attempted to include the true representations and meanings. In common with 'First American', 'Native American' and 'American Indian', I believe my terminology may strike an uneasy compromise, for which I apologize in advance to anybody who might interpret insensitivity.

Whoever you are, and wherever you are, I hope you find this book both enjoyable and useful.

Serle Chapman.

FOREWORD – SONNY SKYHAWK

The plight of our people, our history and lifestyles, have been the subject of many talking papers during the last century, most written with little honour, respect or regard for truth. Not in as many winters has an effort been more noble and deserving of recognition and acknowledgement by our people, than the one you are about to experience by Serle Chapman. He is an Englishman standing on the outside, looking in at an atrocious period of time and, in my opinion, rendering his views and experiences in the most eloquent and beautiful use of the English language. He is a gifted individual who possesses the same heart and spirit as our people, along with the compassion and understanding of the Native American Indian. As a modern day warrior who continues to fight for the human rights, spirituality and dignity of our people, I am honoured to stand and speak on his behalf.

We, as the first inhabitants of this land now called America, have survived unconscionable treatment, such as genocide and oppression, followed by degrading untruths. We shall always have a place of honour in our hearts for those who have the tenacity to seek, and speak the truth about our people. We may never again experience the freedom and innocence of our ancestors, but the truth will be known as long as we have people like Serle Chapman.

As for the future of the Native American Indian, the Creator continues to provide us with strength, inspiration and spiritual guidance, to pass on to our next generations. We still hold in reverence, and honour, what the Creator has given us, the respect and love of Mother Earth. We continue to revere the four-leggeds and wingeds, the trees, the water, the air, the sun and the moon. No one can ever take that away from us, for that is the essence and core of our spirit.

'Mitakuye Oyasin', in my native Lakota language, means 'we are all related in the eyes of the Creator'. Let us hope and pray, as we approach the next millennium, that we treat each other humanely, and with respect and dignity.

Pilámaya Pelo. Thank you.

Looking For My Sister, Miracle

During the Moon When The Cherries Are Dark Red, the White Buffalo Calf Woman brought the Sacred Calf Pipe to the Lakotas, and the Seven Rites in which to use it. She explained how the pipe represented Mother Earth, the four-leggeds who live upon her, all that grow from her, and the wingeds above.
Before leaving, she vowed to return in a time of confusion.
The people watched her walk towards the west, and suddenly she became a young black buffalo that changed colour to red then blonde and finally white.
Nineteen generations later, in 1994, during the Moon When The Cherries Are Dark Red, a white buffalo calf was born. Two years on, 'Miracle' has changed colour from white to black, then red, and blonde.

Pte San Win – Lakota

It's big. In fact, it's really big. Nothing can prepare you for that first time when it's just you, an infinite ribbon of black-top and a prairie that coalesces with the horizon at the edge of the world, all gloved by a sky so blue it would bleed the ocean dry. On that day, every cliché you've ever heard will be true. It is the 'Big Sky', it is a sea of grass, there are snow capped peaks and crystal clear streams, there are many rivers to cross and there was 'gold in them there hills'. When you ask a local how far your next destination is, the answer will be in hours, not miles. The expanse can be daunting, particularly to an Englishman who, at home, can drive from coast to coast, east to west, in under three hours. The concept of driving fifty or sixty miles to the next town, which may only consist of five houses, three shacks, two chickens and a horse, is completely alien. And the prospect of driving the same fifty or sixty miles without seeing another motorist is quite absurd. In England, yes. In the West you'd better get used to the idea. Accept that it's a long way before you set off and enjoy the ride. There is nowhere on earth like the American West.

Even now the prairie keeps its enigmatic promise.

recent that you cannot hide from the sense of pain, the forfeit and conflict, each event and life a microcosm of what became the 'American Dream'. The Little Bighorn, the California Gold Rush, the Transcontinental Railroads, the Washita, the closure of the Bozeman Trail, the ride of John Portugee Phillips, the Oregon and Santa Fe Trails, Pikes Peak or Bust! Which were the triumphs and which the disasters? Red Cloud, John C. Frémont, Manuelito, George Armstrong Custer, Silas Soule, Cochise, Philip Sheridan, Satanta, James Marshall, Sitting Bull, William T. Sherman, Jim Bridger, Geronimo, Wild Bill Hickok, Quanah Parker, Charles Gatewood, Crazy Horse, Kit Carson, Chief Joseph, Lewis and Clark; who were the heroes and who were the villains? In a land of contradictions, in an era when to most, the ends justified any means, the American character was born where the sun always falls.

A truth that all must hold to be self-evident is the prevailing cost of possibly the greatest population expansion in world history. It didn't take Jefferson's '1,000 years', more the belief in John L. O'Sullivan's 'Manifest

GO WEST . . .
YOUNG MAN AND GROW UP WITH THE COUNTRY
Horace Greeley, New York Tribune, 1855

Betrayed though it is by fence posts and wire, what lured men to believe it was forever a beginning is still whispered, albeit softly, between the buttes and draws that swell and tumble beneath the endless plains. Mountains are torn from its belly, impossible red rock sculptures and sandstone fingers impale any suggestion of monotony, and canyons so deep they defeated greed await amidst forests and geysers across the lollipop dunes of painted deserts. This isn't a country or a continent, so far is it beyond a dream.

The land bears scars from much of what is called ambition, the anguish interpreted and preserved by National Parks, Monuments and Historic Sites across the West. The sense of being swallowed by living history is exhilarating, the defining moments of not only the 'Old West' but, in many respects, the entire nation, were so

Destiny'. It took tragedy, sacrifice, fortitude, bravery and wagon loads of blood, sweat and lies drenched in tears. But it was more than that, more than the hapless Donner Party and others whose wheels came off. It took brutality and deceit. Genocide on a scale that is difficult to comprehend.

Emanuel Leutze's painting, 'Westward, The Course Of Empire Takes Its Way', daubes the sky of morality blue. Only those who strained to make the wilderness bloom are triumphantly depicted wielding axes, waving guns and whipping mules. Like the two- and four-leggeds, and the foreboding mountains in Leutze's work, the Native Americans were hazards to be subdued, or eliminated, on the way. 'Where are the warriors today? Who slew them? What law have I broken? Is it wrong for me to love my own? Is it wicked for me because my skin is red?

Because I am a Lakota; because I was born where my father lived; because I would die for my people and my country?' Sitting Bull never received an answer. I often think about a little girl I saw at the Little Bighorn Battlefield who wanted to buy a postcard of Sitting Bull because she thought he looked 'cool'. Her father wouldn't let her. 'Why do you want a picture of a savage?' he asked, as he pulled her away.

When his brother followed the 'Course of Empire', Mark Twain believed he would have '. . . ever such a fine time and write home and tell us all about it . . .'. Twain imagined the contents of that letter, and most popular opinion of the West, and Native Americans, has been 'Cowboys and Indians' ever since.

Throughout most of the nineteenth and twentieth centuries, '*los indios*', 'the Indians', have been portrayed as bloodthirsty savages, cowardly heathens, redskins who would rip your scalp from your head in the blink of an eye. 'The only good Indians I ever saw were dead', spat General Philip Sheridan at a surrendering Comanche in 1868, a sentiment John Ford and his imitators perpetuated and projected across silver screens the world over. People believed it. And worst of all, some still do. Unlike Columbus, these people weren't lost, they knew exactly *where* they were and *who* they were. They weren't '*los indios*', as the disorientated seafarer had christened them, they were individuals from hundreds of sovereign nations whose cultures and philosophies pre-dated the Phoenicians, the Chinese, the Egyptians, and the rise and fall of the Roman Empire. Although diverse in language, custom and appearance, these people shared a creed before the Apostles. They aspired to attain harmony with the natural world, and to protect their Mother, the earth, as guardians of the part that was sacred to them. No man could own what the Creator had provided for all that walked, crawled and flew . . . until the storm broke in the East.

Maybe the truth became too painful to recognize. I don't imagine that John Wayne would have been quite so popular if the scriptwriters had wanted him to say that the 'Land of the Free' came from conquest and subjugation. Hollywood eased the conscience of America by reinventing the continent's history and, in the process, created stereotypes beneath a veil of racism that in a stroke degraded and dehumanized Native Americans. Naturally, it wouldn't have been entertaining to make a movie about how 90 per cent of the indigenous peoples who populated the continent before the European invasion were exterminated through warfare, starvation and imported diseases in the proceeding three hundred years. And it would have taken all of a studio's orange make-up and supply of long black wigs, not to mention an expansive cast of monosyllabic white actors to wear them, to tell how the Great Law of the Iroquois, 'Kaianerekowa', influenced Benjamin Franklin's Albany Plan of Union for the British Colonies, and then the Founding Fathers, who studied the League of the Iroquois before pronouncing the Constitution of the United States Government in 1789.

Chimney Rock, Nebraska

Clarks Fork, Montana

No, that would never have made a good movie, particularly the bit about how the Founding Fathers omitted the fundamental Iroquois principle of equality amongst all men and both genders. Now, if a director could have persuaded Audrey Hepburn to play Tsakaka-wias, the Shoshone woman without whose diplomacy Lewis and Clark would have failed to reach the Pacific coast from St Louis, Missouri, the movie moguls might have been on to something. 'Fort Clatsop and Back' . . . well, perhaps not, it doesn't roll off the tongue like *The Unforgiven*. And Hollywood could always argue that white American patriots were pretending to be 'Indians' before the War of Independence, 'remember the Boston Tea Party?'

It is easy to forget that the Frontier was once the Atlantic coastline, not west of the Mississippi. 'Thanksgiving' is a Wampanoag custom that was adopted by the Pilgrims who sailed into Patuxet Harbour and renamed it 'Plymouth' in 1620. After the harvest of 1621 those same Pilgrims gave thanks to their Puritan God, not Tisquantum (Patuxet Nation), Samoset (Abenaki Nation) or Massasoit (Wampanoag Nation), the men who had taught them how to survive and cultivate the crops they celebrated. The Wampanoags were rewarded with slavery and death, the head of Massasoit's son, Metacom, was displayed on a stake in Plymouth Harbour because he refused to submit.

The Wampanoag, 'The People Of The First Light', are Algonquian speakers, along with the Cheyenne, Blackfeet, Shawnee, Powhatan, Cree and numerous others. The term 'caucus' is derived from the Algonquian languages and the origins of the contemporary political convention are traditionally Native American. It was an Algonquian alliance of Sauk and Mesquakie guided by Black Hawk, who fought to protect their sacred lands west of the Wabash River against a United States force that included Lieutenant Jefferson Davis and Captain Abraham Lincoln. When some of the stars fell from the stripes into the bars twenty-nine years later, the armies of Presidents Lincoln and Davis welcomed the twenty thousand Native American volunteers who died for the bluecoats and grey. Hasa-no-anda, a Tonawanda Seneca sachem known as Colonel Ely Parker, drew up the terms of General Lee's surrender. Two months after Lee had signed, Stand Watie, Chief Degadoga of the Cherokee Nation (South), was the last Confederate General to hand his sword and pledge to the Union. Abraham Lincoln once said that history is the one thing from which there is no escape.

Someday you may be on an American Indian Reservation, surrounded by hardship. When you're there and you're shocked by the material poverty, will you think of the movies or will you recall the history that developed into the fabric of the United States? Will you admire these people for surviving invasion and deception, persecution that included, but is by no means restricted to, the fraudulent exploitation of the Proclamation of 1763 and the Ordinance Regulations of 1786/87, the Indian Removal Act, the Dawes General Allotment Act, the Curtis 'tribal termination' Act, religious prohibition, and

Delicate Arch, Utah

Monument Valley, Arizona

the federally supported enforced assimilation of the 'Indian' boarding school regime that championed Richard Henry Pratt's motto 'Kill the Indian and Save the Man'. Will you see that, or will you only notice ramshackled trailers, tired looking buildings and cars that have seen better days? I'm not telling you there aren't problems, there are and they are numerous. I am only asking you to disregard

Honour – Crow Fair

the misconceptions. The Native Americans are neither dead nor dying, they are still fighting, struggling for recognition and striving to preserve their culture and heritage. Reservations are currently people's homes, not parks or curiosities, and photography is often inappropriate, particularly of sacred sites. If in doubt, ask, and seek the meaning of crass terms such as 'redskin' and 'squaw' before you even think about using them.

The central bond between man and all of creation that I perceive to be the pulse of Native American spirituality inspired this book. That everything in the universe is of spirit, and all within it are created equal, unites the heart to the light of the soul. The Lakota say Mitakuye Oyasin,

'All My Relations', the two-leggeds, the four-leggeds and the wings of the air, the animate and inanimate. If you believe that man possesses dominion over the earth and all that share it, you should reconsider before walking in the shadow of the bear and elk. There you will begin to appreciate Mitakuye Oyasin and realise that words such as 'wild' and 'beast', and the trepidation draped around them, were created by man to manipulate men into being scared of the dark, when in truth, there was only ever light.

It was always about dreams. The clash of cultures and fight for the land was a collision of ideals, the will to possess over that to preserve. From the east they conquered to make reality the order of society today. But as we languish in the relative comfort of certainty, our lives dictated by artificial demand, we think of how it was and wish that, if only for one day, there were no fence posts and wire. Go West! Not through the persuasion of a latter day Horace Greeley, but with a passion that allows you to believe. Never say 'It was only a dream'.

Once Upon A Time In The West

We did not think of the great open plains, the beautiful rolling hills,
and winding streams with tangled growth, as 'wild'.
Only to the white man was nature a 'wilderness',
and only to him was the land 'infested' with 'wild animals' and 'savage' people . . .
When the very animals of the forest began fleeing from his approach,
then it was that for us the 'Wild West' began.

Standing Bear – Lakota
Land Of The Spotted Eagle

Gray Wolf

I stared down upon it from the gleaming ramparts and wondered how it was for them. It looked placid to me, tamed as it is by concrete and steel, but when it dictated and its mood changed, I wondered how it was then, this river, or myth, called the Mississippi. A sense of misguided loyalty nagged me to spare a thought for the trappers and traders who had dared it, then plundered, all for the coin of the realm, before where I was standing, Fort Snelling, Minnesota, had symbolically prized control of the fur trade from Britain's grasp. Obligation satisfied, I felt no empathy with those who had, in reality, bribed for King and Country, or their foes who seven years after the victory of 1812 laboured for another six to build Colonel Josiah Snelling's outpost above Mendota. When I wondered how it was, it wasn't for the 5th Regiment of US Infantry but the women they dragged along to work under a regime that surely seemed close to hell. For them it must have been love because for once there was no ulterior motive.

How the Chippewa, Menominee and Santee Dakotas felt about the Long Knives replacing the Red Coats I cannot imagine. By then, did it matter? Instead of the British, it was the *American* and *Columbia* fur companies who bloated in the cradle of Fort Snelling and the adjoining St Peter's Agency. Trading furs for guns, blankets, cloth, beads, kettles, knives, mirrors and awls may have made their presence tolerable, until the seduction of greed and alcohol became part of the bargain and smallpox and tuberculosis were distributed without treaty or charge.

Where once they wouldn't have been so hard to find, those that became bounty now lay to the north of Fort Snelling, beyond the shores of Lake Superior in the sanctuary of the Superior National Forest. Imposing and vehement in cause, today the woodland strains to clutch what encroachment grudgingly concedes. I went there to see two who have suffered more than most. The first ran from me. He was beautiful, of course, but he didn't know my feelings or what I believed in, he couldn't take the chance. He'd been lied to, betrayed by the hand that once fed him, and his father and mother, and theirs before, taught him to beware of the one that cannot be trusted. I understood why he couldn't take the chance, after all, we all look and smell the same.

WEST, ACROSS THE MISSISSIPPI

We were once as brothers but though forever the progenitor of our 'best friend', he lives in the twilight and shade, concealed by the forest in a bid to survive the lies that have screamed hate. He's beautiful, of course, like Shakespeare on a bitter night, his song and his plea beseech an answer. Here his voice is one of twelve hundred but away from this forest the wolf's silence is

Otter

I fear for them because trust is still possible. In a short space of time I became familiar to some, so close that I could smell the sweet aroma from their fur warmed by the late summer sun . . . and on others the stench of the hunters' bait congealed around their necks and ears. In that moment, *our* moment, when there are no guns; inside what humans call vulnerability, you share

rarely broken, at most another hundred howl across the lower forty-eight states. Those who would listen should do so first at the International Wolf Centre in Ely.

It was cold when they left me. I didn't notice until they had gone. The trees looked bigger that morning, suspending dawn for a while longer and handing gold to the lake and the otters' fleet shine. Teasing, the occasional 'plop' from exuberance slapped the water and gave their game away but the surface barely sighed as they slid past without encore. Here in the forest and on the many shores, the Chippewa must have watched, as I did, and wished for the otter's grace. The divine caller, Manabôzhô, gave the otter-spirit to the Chippewa and other Algonquians who followed the Midê. Guided by the otter, the Midêwiwin Grand Medicine Society learnt the mystery, dreams and phenomena of the natural world and what it was to be reborn. Entry to the Midê required purity of conduct and heart, the initiate viewed like the muskrat or beaver, on the trail of sacred ways embodied by the bear, the second I'd travelled to see.

'And by the river there's a big ol' black bear', the receptionist kept telling me in the months before I arrived. It wasn't a lie. I was welcomed by his skin, spread-eagled and nailed to the cabin wall. The 'Rogue of the River' had been too early, or was it I who was too late? I left without speaking, knowing that if I stayed there could be no honesty between his kind and mine. But I did find them, powerful and proud until they saw me and fled, deep into the long shadows, wary of the scent that harbours the gun.

honour and truth. You wait and you watch and you reach out to touch the spirit that the bear has granted. In those seconds of faith all that has gone before seems forgiven. Hope is a glade at the end of a dirt track fostered by boughs and leaves. And without the Vince Shute Wildlife Sanctuary, Orr would be a town along the roadside waiting for the stop-light and weather to change before watching for red and the rain again.

I wonder if it is always a surprise to see Duluth belching and coughing on the tip of Superior's western shore. Maybe the military man and trader who shared its name used to do the same. Whatever, Duluth fits on the map better than 'One Wrong Turn And You're In Wisconsin'. Duluth was one of the first to produce an ethnographic interpretation of the people the Chippewa called nadowe-ssi-wag, 'the snake-like ones', or 'enemies', that on a French tongue became 'nadouessioux', then simply 'The Sioux'. Those the French first stumbled across in a village of bark cabins near Mille Lacs would have called themselves 'Dakota', the 'Allied'. They were the Mdewakanton, the 'People of the Spirit Lake Village', and the heart of their Creation lay where the two great rivers converge on Mendota.

The first official representative of the United States to meet the Mdewakanton was Lieutenant Zebulon Pike, who left them holding $200 worth of trade goods and liquor in return for a treaty ceding one hundred thousand acres of land. The Europeans had sailed up the river for years but they left it to the Americans to finally sell the Dakotas down it.

He's beautiful, of course — Wolf

Crossing at the point the Dakotas describe as 'The Place Where The Water Falls', Minneapolis, I remember Zebulon Pike. At the time of his contact with the Mdewakanton, Pike discovered that 'The Sioux' were a confederation of constituent tribes known as the Oceti Sakowin, the 'Seven Council Fires'. The Mdewakanton, along with the other Dakota speakers, the Wahpeton, Sisseton and Wahpekute, represented four of those as the Santee Dakota, with the collectively termed Teton Lakota, and the Yankton Nakota/Dakota Wiciyela divisions, completing the alliance. Despite his insight, Pike's comment that the Wahpekutes 'Were the most stupid and inactive of all the Sioux' proved, at best, to be misguided. Led by Inkpaduta, the Wahpekutes were the first to rebel against the settlers before the Minnesota Sioux War.

Between here and Interstate 90 I have to drive through Mankato and as hard as I try to hide behind every radio station the search button skips by, my mind will not relinquish the torment of that war or what occurred. I have no idea why I feel that way about something that happened one hundred and four years before I was born. The Dakotas fought in Tecumseh's Shawnee alliance alongside the British in the War of 1812, but the Red Coats didn't reciprocate when asked, as they had promised to do. In 1862, 15 per cent of the reservation Dakotas had English, Scottish or French ancestry, most being children or grandchildren of traders who had 'married' into Dakota families to ensure that they would control the village's trade.

The United States government encouraged traders to entice the 'Sioux' into procuring huge debts, content that the inevitable demands for repayment would leave them no alternative but to sign government treaties in return for the money to pay those arrears. In 1851 the Dakotas did that. Having given up 26 million acres of land for money the government paid direct to the traders, and meagre annuities to subsist on the barren plots onto which they had been pushed, victory for the Dakotas became survival. By August 1862 they were starving. Their annual allotments hadn't arrived and the traders severed all credit. 'If they are hungry, let them eat grass or their own dung', scoffed one, Andrew Myrick. Even though the Indian Agency warehouses were stocked with their provisions, the government agent, Thomas Galbraith, refused to distribute them before the annuity funds arrived. Incensed, the Dakotas walked out of the Redwood Council and into the 'Minnesota Sioux War'.

Bull Moose

Hysterical accounts of the three month conflict followed, and the scalp the army and settlers wanted most belonged to Ta-eo-duta, 'His Red Nation', a sixty-year-old Mdewakanton leader known as 'Little Crow' who, on the day of the outbreak, had attended the Lower Agency Episcopal Church. To the last he spoke for peace but when his own people called him a coward for not wanting to fight, he led them out of, and into, desperation.

Over three hundred and ninety-two Dakota men were tried for participating in the war, the trials having proceeded at a rate of one prisoner every ten minutes. The press criticized the commission for dragging its heels but

Alpha Male – Wolf

stateline into South Dakota, but for Little Crow the journey took one hundred and eight years. He was shot while picking raspberries with his son on 3 July 1863. The Minnesota Legislature paid the farmer who killed him $500 for his scalp, plus the regular Sioux scalp bounty of $25, then placed it on display along with his bones in St Paul. Little Crow was finally laid to rest at Flandreau, South Dakota, after his remains were removed from the museum shelf in 1971. The only consolation may be that he lies within reach of the Sacred Pipestone Quarry, where once a great flood swept across the plains. Thousands drowned in the flood and their flesh and blood became the sacred red pipestone. Forever after, the pipestone was smoked as a symbol of peace by the people of the Oceti Sakowin. Some say it happened that way, but through my eyes forever is now yellow between Flandreau and the Badlands. The plains that sustain the ranches and farms, the light on bashful settlements perched atop roadside knolls. I even hear yellow in the meadowlark's song.

Imagine the ruins of Pompeii dropped onto the plains and you'll get a crude picture of the Badlands. Serrated from the blade of frost, wind and rain, carnivorous jaws prise the prairie open to bare razor-sharp ridges and menacing spurs that have been slashed from layers of sandstone over sixty-five million years old. Yuccas pierce the fractured slopes and short grasses scratch around slivers of sediment flaking from blistered canyon floors. Laced by cottonwoods and wild roses which spin green threads across the corrugated terrain, as inhospitable as it appears, the Badlands brutality can deceive. Prairie dogs twitch and chatter by their burrows like nervous commuters waiting for a late train, while buzzards, coyotes, hawks and bobcats hope it never arrives. Rocky Mountain bighorn sheep pick precarious trails over crumbling ledges jutting from cliff walls, and mule deer scour crevasses and draws at dusk and dawn. On the mesas pronghorn antelope bucks groom before impressionable does. Indifferent to their performances, in Sage Creek Basin, the buffalo watch them come and go.

The Teton Lakota Nations; the Oglalas, Mnikowojus, Sicangus, Hunkpapas, Sihasapas, Oohenunpas and Itazipcos; gave the Badlands its name, and their history cuts through 'mako sica' deeper than any of the ravines or gullies. It was here, to the O-ona-gashee, the 'Sheltering Place' in the Stronghold Table, that those who survived the Wounded Knee massacre fled to make *their* last stand.

were appeased when three hundred and three Dakotas were condemned to die, and their families imprisoned within the walls that had been built upon the sacred land of Mendota. On 26 December 1862, thirty-eight climbed the gallows in Mankato. The spectators felt cheated because so many sentences had been commuted, but then welcomed the greatest mass execution in American history during the week that President Lincoln issued the emancipation proclamation. Leaving Mankato I imagine their cheers. It's 1995 and I wonder if the orderly yards and houses notice as another country music station whistles by.

For me it will only take a couple of hours to cross the

You can stop at Big Foot Pass and attempt to put yourself in the place of one of those who trekked the one hundred and fifty miles by pony and foot through the vagaries of that Dakota Territory winter. Pursued by fear after Sitting Bull's murder, and hunted by the army for practising the Ghost Dance, Big Foot's band of one hundred and twenty men, and two hundred and thirty women

Mako Sica

and children, had accepted Red Cloud's invitation to join the Oglala Lakotas on the Pine Ridge Reservation. At Porcupine Butte in the Badlands they were intercepted by the 7th Cavalry. Major Samuel Whitside refused to parley with any of the Mnikowoju or Hunkpapa Lakotas except for Chief Big Foot who, already suffering from pneumonia, had started haemorrhaging. Under a flag of truce Big Foot was assured that if he surrendered and his people followed the soldiers to their camp, they would not be harmed.

With Hotchkiss guns trained on their lodges, the Lakota refugees camped on Chankpe Opi Wakpala, 'The Creek Called Wounded Knee', as Colonel James W. Forsyth assumed command of the 7th Cavalry and celebrated their capture by cracking open a keg of whisky with his men. The Lakotas were to be disarmed and Big Foot shipped to prison in Omaha. When morning came the Lakotas set their weapons down, aware that

some of the soldiers surrounding them were veterans from Custer's 7th who fourteen years earlier had escaped from the Little Bighorn. As the soldiers ransacked their lodges and ordered them to drop their blankets to be body searched, Yellow Bird, a holy man, told them not to be afraid, 'The prairie is large and their bullets will not find you', he mumbled in Lakota, shuffling a few steps from the Ghost Dance. One young Mnikowoju warrior heard neither Yellow Bird or the command to submit his weapon. Black Coyote was deaf. The soldiers grabbed his Winchester but he wouldn't release it and, as they wrestled it from his grasp, the gun discharged a single shot. A few minutes later the bodies of two hundred and fifty Lakotas were heaped, like their weapons, amongst the shreds of their camp. The women and children who ran were pursued and hacked down in the muddy coulees.

When all fell silent, the wounded were bundled into a wagon and left outside the agency church in a biting frost. Eventually they were taken inside and told to rest on the hay that had been thrown around the floor. Drooping from the pulpit above them was a banner that read 'Peace on Earth, Goodwill to All Men'. The fourth day of Christmas 1890 was about to end.

Pronghorn Antelope

While Old Man was in the mountains He created the antelope,
but it stumbled on the rocks as it ran.
'This will not do', He said, when the antelope fell, so He led it down to the prairie.
'This is what you are suited to', Old Man told the antelope,
and gave it the freedom of the plains.

Blackfeet

Bighorn Ram

Nearly three hundred Mnikowojus and Hunkpapas had died. Two days later, stripped by the soldiers for souvenirs, their frozen bodies were tossed into a mass grave. Between the 'Congressional Medals of Honor' awarded to the 7th Cavalry for their 'bravery', twenty-five of their number had perished, ostensibly from 'friendly fire'. A single monument naming the Lakotas who were massacred now stands among modest graves overlooking the killing field. Wiping the tears of seven generations, and laying Lakota foundations for the following seven, in 1990 three hundred riders of the Oceti Sakowin endured temperatures of 30° below zero to retrace the Hunkpapas and Mnikowojus tragic journey to Wounded Knee on the Big Foot Memorial Ride.

West of the Badlands the plains erupt. Inching towards the setting sun, silhouetted mounds bubble from the short cropped table top. The closer you get, the steeper the mass of peaks until the charcoal sketch of distance is brushed aside by bold green strokes. Silence isn't lonesome in the Black Hills, it's just part of a different song. Lakota genesis tells of a song that was given to the universe upon creation. Each part of the universe learnt a verse of that song, but the entire song can only be heard here, in the Black Hills. When there was only darkness, Inyan, The Rock, inflicted a wound on his body to create life for others. His blood was blue and flowed from him to form the waters, the shape of the earth and the lifeforce that inspired the sky. The world was born, like all life, from generosity and pain, and that sacrifice for life is honoured in the Sun Dance when the people shed their blood so that the earth and all upon it may continue to breathe and be renewed. Nowhere is that vow more poignant than in the Black Hills. In the beginning it looks as though the heavens burst and rained splinters of granite that penetrated the slopes before a wandering forest of Black Hills spruce, Aspen and Ponderosa pine sprang from the earth to dress the once bald mountains.

Paha Sapa, or He˙ Sapa, the Black Hills, have always been the 'Heart Of Everything That Is' for the Lakota. In terms of a spiritual perspective, think of the significance the

Black Bear

Lord's Prayer has to Christians '. . . thy kingdom come, thy will be done, on earth as it is in heaven'. And then consider the Lakota view that the stars are the 'holy breath' of Wakan Tanka, the Creator of the 'Heart of Everything That Is', and that the constellations are visible scriptures that mirror prominent sites within the Black Hills, making what is on earth, the Black Hills, also in heaven and vice versa. In common with all theological belief, be it Christian, Apache, Islam or any other, there is no short-cut to document Lakota. Even so, I still found it strange that at the 'Cave Of The Winds', now Wind Cave National Monument, visitors are readily informed about Jesse and Tom Bingham 'discovering' the cave in 1881, but no mention is made of the Lakota's belief that the wolf and Tokahe, the first man, led the Lakotas from the Buffalo Nation onto the face of the earth through the cave. I accept that those who have recorded the history of the American West are of the opinion that 'The Sioux' were forced westward onto the prairie by the Chippewa and that, upon arriving in the Black Hills, they dispossessed the Kiowa. Now I'm sure that when you've driven thousands of miles across the United States to stand before Mount Rushmore and marvel at the 'shrine of democracy', that's a perfectly acceptable analysis, something along the lines of 'well, they pushed out somebody else and we just did the same to them'. I suppose some think that's alright, but unless credence is given to the views of both the pushers and the pushed it's certainly not democratic. I would never demean Gutzon Borglum's artistry, or what his sculpture means to those who gaze up at it hand on heart singing the *Star Spangled Banner*. Borglum's intention was for the monument to represent American ideals, a memorial dedicated to freedom and democracy. But hand on heart, I ask you how that can be possible when in 1980 the US Supreme Court upheld the Lakota's treaty claims, filed as Docket 74-B. The Court decreed that 'A more ripe and rank case of dishonorable dealing will never, in all probability, be found in our history', ruling that the United States Government had violated the 1868 Fort Laramie Treaty when it unlawfully seized the Black Hills from the 'Sioux Nation', in 1877. Surely all of those who pay homage to celebrate democracy would welcome the opportunity to see that treaty and subsequent judgement displayed within the Mount Rushmore Visitors' Centre, with the history, and present, interpreted from a Lakota perspective. What does it profit a man to gain the world and lose his soul?

Wild Turkey

that the prophet Motseyoef, 'Sweet Medicine', collected the Sacred Arrows for the Cheyenne, and then brought them the Massaum, the 'wonderful dance'. On the day I sat looking towards the prayer ties hanging from the trees, a man who was closer to sixty than forty told me that the Kiowas had received the power of the bear on this 'Sacred Mountain Where People Are Taught'. He asked me where I was from, then returned the favour. He had family near Lame Deer, Montana, but was from Oklahoma. I wanted to ask him about his people, the Southern Cheyenne, but I thought it would be intrusive. We talked for a while but were comfortably silent as much as we spoke. Before I left he smiled and said, 'Not everybody can hear well up here on Nowah'wus', and that's what I remember most. The 'maiyun' spirits who walk through the seven realms of the universe communicate with the Cheyenne on Nowah'wus and show themselves upon the earth as the wolf, the buffalo, badger and bear.

Sometimes I feel the touch of pathos, at others overwhelming irony, that Mount Rushmore will eventually be surpassed by Korczak Ziolkowski's colossal mountain carving of Crazy Horse. Ziolkowski worked fleetingly with Borglum on Mount Rushmore, but at the request of Lakota Chief, Henry Standing Bear, began Crazy Horse in 1949 with only $174 between his bank account and pockets. Independent of state and federal funds, the ultimate objective is for 'Crazy Horse' to overlook an educational complex that includes the 'University and Medical Training Centre of the North American Indian'. Occasionally I wonder what the venerated Oglala visionary and warrior would have made of it all. In life he was dedicated to the preservation of his people and the land upon which they lived. An introverted, modest man who shunned attention, after his murder at Fort Robinson, Nebraska on 5 September 1877, might his spirit have felt that the beauty of Hè Sapa was enough, and that natural wonders like Bear Butte were living testimony to his and other souls departed.

In a way it began and ended near Bear Butte. With the sun yawning sooner on twilight's unfolding stage, Crazy Horse was born on Rapid Creek as the Lakotas drifted away from their council at Bear Butte in the year of the Big Horse Steal. If the land were pregnant Bear Butte would be the distended womb. Sacred and serene, its ambience never challenges but shares the great mystery with the Lakotas and Cheyennes who make the Vision Quest. It was here

So typical of the West, it was the consequence of what happened here that left so many Lakotas and Cheyennes heartbroken. On 15 August 1874, his camp in the shadow of Bear Butte, Brevet Major General George Armstrong Custer completed his Black Hills Expedition report. In French Creek, near the present day town of Custer, H. N. Ross had discovered what the government sent Custer to look for . . . GOLD. Custer wrote that there was 'gold among the grass roots and in paying quantities in every stream'. When his intimidating military column clattered back across the plains to Fort Abraham Lincoln, North Dakota, Custer had not only contravened the Treaty of 1868 but furrowed the Thieves Road for the government and thousands of prospectors to exploit. In the summer of 1876 Custer marched out of Fort Abraham Lincoln for the last time, heading beyond the Powder River country to finish what he had started.

Black Bear

My fur has touched you, so you shall live to be brave.

My paws have touched your hands, so you shall have the strength of a great warrior.

My mouth passes wisdom to yours, so you shall use it to lead your people.

For these things give thanks to Tiráwa, the Creator, who gave us the power to save you.

The Bear's gift of life to Bear Man – Pawnee

Red Cloud– Hè Sapa

To the Drum and Heart

HÈ SAPA

The Seventh Direction is the Heart of Everything That Is.
The spotted eagle above, the spider below, the Thunders in the West, the Morning Star in the East,
the magpie and the meadowlark on the winds North and South,
all gather at the fire in the tipi, around the human heart,
and the heart of Earth – Hè Sapa.

The Black Hills – Lakota

Bull Buffalo

25 June '96 – Still Standing

Bull Buffalo

I have heard my brothers, the dog and owl,

and I shall also help you.

I give you my strength and endurance,

and the protection of my hide.

Pledge of the Bull Buffalo – Young Dog Society
Cree

Grizzly Bear

Doleful in teardrop eyes, they squint into the wind. Be they stampeding, plodding or idly ruminating, they always seem to face the wind. Their scraggly beards begin artless two-steps in rhythm with chewing cud as they wait for passengers to land on their backs and peck out fares of ticks and flies. Flapping languidly, shaggy pantaloons make them look weary to the trot, the lethargy accentuated by each of the wobbling woolly heads that step after step bob along as if dangling from a puppeteer's strings. Suddenly their tails rise and a herd of chocolate and gingerbread humps skim like fins through waves of prairie grass with lanky red calves dodging follow the leader between thunderheads of dust and hooves. The blind leading the blind in unforseen panic to the bow and lance, then insatiable gun.

Sit tight if you're close enough to eavesdrop on them griping about this and that, their vocabulary blunt and rounded, dipping between grunts and lows. I was privvy to their gossip once but as intoxicating as it was, I wouldn't recommend it unless you're short on after-dinner conversation. My companions and I had been trailing a band of pronghorn antelope across some open terrain.

To the people of the plains the buffalo was everything; a generous provider of food and clothing, shelter for their homes, weapons, utensils and fuel. The buffalo was, and for most still is, sacred, the embodiment of spiritual and ceremonial symbolism. It was the White Buffalo Woman who brought the Buffalo Calf Pipe to the Lakota people and the Seven Rites in which to use it that became the soul of the nation, a bond between man and every aspect of Wakan Tanka. The white buffalo walks divine but in the scramble for control of the continent others saw it differently. 'The hide hunters will do more to settle the vexed Indian question than the entire regular army has done . . . They are destroying the Indians' commissary . . . Let them kill, skin and sell until the buffaloes are exterminated', proclaimed General Philip Sheridan, then commander of US troops on the plains, a belief advocated by General William T. Sherman, who defined the Union Pacific Railroad's charge along the Platte River as instrumental in that common cause. At that time the last unmolested buffalo range of the Lakotas and their allies lay between the Black Hills and the Bighorn Mountains, the

BEYOND THE POWDER RIVER COUNTRY

Ordinarily you might expect to notice five hundred bison wandering towards you and, of course, we did, they just happened to be about twenty feet away by the time they had acquired our undivided attention. We stood still and they paid us no mind until one particular cow decided that we might observe them with less distraction from a better vantage point. When I turned around I was surprised to see that our back marker had vanished. Then I noticed the buffalo tossing its head up and down below an adjacent tree, with my friend perched in it. Eventually the cow trotted away with the others and we watched them settle in the distance. As the sun slipped behind the Black Hills it was almost a dream. A scene from the moon's shadow, more than one hundred years past.

Powder River country of Wyoming and Montana.

Like an old man's withered arms, the Yellowstone and Belle Fourche Rivers are outstretched in welcome across the land. On the map it looks the same as any other embrace but when you are there you understand why people died for its affection. There are places in Wyoming and Montana that exceed the routine limitations of our minds: Devil's Tower, The Bighorn Mountains; Yellowstone, Grand Teton and Glacier National Parks; Lolo Pass, The Shoshone National Forest, Chief Joseph Scenic Highway, and the Northern Rockies among them. And dotted amidst the rapture are the theatres of suffering and glory that all the myths and legends cannot disguise from bloody war. Few keep more secrets than the heart that is the wrinkled country within that old man's breast.

Mule Deer Fawn

Those who summoned the courage to run the gauntlet of Lakota and Cheyenne resistance along the Bozeman Trail initially made Montana unscathed by pacifying the warriors with a toll of black medicine and sweet white lumps. In 1864 upwards of one thousand settlers and prospectors took the road and gave away a lot of coffee, but for the government that wasn't enough. General Patrick E. Connor was dispatched to bring the 'wolves' to heel, and ordered his men to ignore any peaceful gestures and 'kill every male Indian over twelve years old'. Connor's onslaught on the Powder River country succeeded in outraging the Lakotas and Cheyennes, and his attack on Chief Black Bear's peaceful Arapahos on the Tongue River destroyed not only the village and all they possessed, but also the last fragile remnants of goodwill toward the whites who encroached upon the Powder River. I've sat on that battlefield twice and tried to piece together the fragments of what occurred but on both occasions I have failed. Knowing that women and children were cut down indiscriminately in Connor's assault, I've found it difficult to make sense of the swings and picnic tables that now stand on the battleground in Ranchester City Park.

Connor believed he had partially accomplished the campaign's objectives, he had pitched into the Arapaho women and children, and organized a military post on the Powder River that, in recognition of such grand achievements, he named Fort Connor. By the time Colonel Henry B. Carrington arrived on 28 June 1866, Connor's rickety collection of cottonwood lean-tos had been retitled Fort Reno. Carrington's orders were to fortify the post and then secure control of the Powder River country by constructing two additional forts along the Bozeman Trail. Fourteen days earlier he had marched into Fort Laramie during the government's Peace Commission and found E. B. Taylor trying to negotiate a way out of a previous treaty that ceded the area to the Powder River nations as 'Indian Territory'. Taylor had made no mention of the army's intention to build two more forts in their hunting grounds but Carrington had already stated his purpose to a Sicangu Lakota Chief, Standing Elk. Indignant at the commissioner's deceit, Red Cloud of the Oglala Lakotas pronounced, 'The Great Father sends us presents and wants us to sell him the road, but the white chief goes with soldiers to steal the road before the Indians say Yes or No'. What history calls 'Red Cloud's War' had begun.

Interstate 90 bisects the Powder River country. On its ascent north at the town of Buffalo, Wyoming, I90 obscures the old Montana Road that creeps along beside it through Banner, Bighorn, Beckton and Dayton. Not many give it a second glance, that trail to Montana John Bozeman and John Jacobs chartered in 1864, but in the proceeding year, after four years of Civil War, it left a glint in the government's eye. The Bozeman Trail was the fastest route to Virginia City and the Montana goldfields. With the US Treasury teetering on bankruptcy, the more prospectors who had direct access to the waiting gold, the better it was for adjusting the national debt.

Approximately two hundred miles southeast of the Powder River country, Fort Laramie was arguably the most significant post on the frontier, not least because it shepherded the Oregon Trail. Today it is one of the best National Park Service Historic Sites in the West. In common with the majority of National Monuments and Historic Sites in Wyoming and Montana, Laramie's maintenance, orientation and presentation is second to none. Along from 'Old Bedlam', once home to the fort's bachelor officers, is a marker dedicated to John 'Portugee' Phillips. Phillips rode two hundred and thirty-six miles from the Powder River to Fort Laramie in four days, arriving on Christmas Day 1866 with a dispatch from Colonel Carrington that reported the army's defeat in the pivotal engagement of 'Red Cloud's War'.

In an idyllic location twenty miles south of the authentic western town of Sheridan and five miles north of the Fort Phil Kearny Museum, a gentle ridge huddles between the Bighorn Mountains to the west and fractured plains in the east. Sheltered by the smooth, almost listless, Sullivant Hills that slide into Lodge Trail Ridge, this innocuous fold of land that from a distance looks like a crease in an unmade bed, was the scene of the US Army's second worst military defeat in Plains Warfare. The Cheyenne refer to it as the 'Hundred Soldiers Killed Fight', to the Lakota it is 'A Hundred In The Hands'. The Americans remember it as 'The Fetterman Massacre'.

On a plateau above what the Lakotas called 'Pine Woods', Colonel Carrington meticulously supervised the construction of Fort Phil Kearny, then directed two companies of infantry northwest into Montana to establish Fort C. F. Smith on the Bighorn River. Even though he had garrisoned The Bozeman Trail, reports of a massing Indian encampment and their raids upon the golden road alarmed Carrington. With an inadequate force he was both reluctant to intervene and vulnerable to the developing siege. Reinforcements appeared in the shape of Captain William J. Fetterman and one company of cavalry. 'With eighty men I could ride through the entire Sioux Nation', the young Captain had boasted on his arrival. What became known as the 'Fetterman Massacre' might more accurately be recorded as the 'Fetterman Miscalculation'.

Carrington's logistical weakness at Fort Phil Kearny was having to send a detail five miles from the fort to collect wood, a deficiency the Lakotas and Cheyennes planned to exploit. On 6 December a small decoy party of warriors

Buffalo Cow

attacked the wood train to entice the soldiers out of the fort and into an ambush. Colonel Carrington commanded the relief column and, had some from the phalanx not broken cover, he may have been beguiled. Two weeks later Red Cloud's camp moved closer to Fort Phil Kearny. At dusk on 20 December the leaders asked a Mnikowoju Lakota visionary, Crazy Mule, to seek a prophecy for the impending battle. Eventually, this man who dressed and lived like a woman and was respected for having the foresight of both sexes, returned saying he had 'a hundred soldiers in his hands'. The following morning the established plan was executed with greater precision.

Captain Fetterman insisted on being given command of the relief column and, reluctantly, Carrington agreed but twice gave him explicit orders not to pursue the warriors over Lodge Trail Ridge. Fetterman bolted from Fort Kearny with eighty-one men, one more than he had claimed he needed. When the Lakotas saw him in range they broke away from the woodcutters, leaving a decoy party to taunt Fetterman, who could not resist the challenge. With his infantry lagging behind, he lurched over Lodge Trail Ridge into Peno Valley where, from both sides of what is now called Prairie Dog Creek, the Lakotas, Cheyennes and Arapahos charged from behind every rock and thicket and out of the frosty ravines, the drumming of their hearts as they waited for the moment drowned by the breaking ice that freed the hustling stream.

It was over within forty minutes. Captains Fetterman and Brown saved their last bullets for themselves. Only Dapple Dave, a cavalry mount, was found alive but even he was fatally wounded. The totality of the defeat shocked not only Carrington's detachment but the army, government, and when the news broke, the entire American population. The army survived the proceeding Wagon Box and Hayfield Fights but with the Union Pacific Railroad stalking ever closer to the Central Pacific, the government decided to abandon its Bozeman Trail policy and sent peace commissioners out once more. Red Cloud would not discuss terms until the Powder River forts were abandoned, and in the summer of 1868 the government acquiesced to his demands. Though ratified by the Senate, it is doubtful that the government ever intended to comply with the Fort Laramie Treaty of 1868, the most flagrant violation of which was the catalyst for the army's greatest military defeat, above the banks of the Little Bighorn River.

The Powder River conflict provides a telling insight into the opposing perceptions of that crucial era. General William T. Sherman, a Civil War hero destined to become

Bald Eagle

General in Chief of the US Army, was one of the architects of the 1868 Fort Laramie Treaty. Sherman represented a government and people whose approach toward the continent's original inhabitants was either 'civilize' or 'exterminate'. Their opinions differed but their conquest remained the same; both wanted to dispossess the Native Americans, the majority just didn't want the trouble of putting ploughs in their hands, cutting their hair and imposing the word of Christ upon them.

Sherman knew that invading the Lakota's and Cheyenne's sacred hunting grounds would deflect them from the railroad and incite an open war which, when his forts were built, he assumed the army would win. Alongside other similarly inappropriate officers, Carrington and Fetterman were chosen to instigate this subjugation. Colonel Carrington had no combat experience, while Fetterman had fought throughout Sherman's Georgia Campaign of 1864. It is probable that the nearest either of them had been to a Lakota or Cheyenne warrior was a Catlin or Bodmer painting. History has painted Fetterman as an arrogant fool. Certainly he was arrogant and impetuous but was he brave or stupid? In certain situations is there a difference? His Civil War record was impeccable, having been cited for gallantry at Stone's River. His prejudices were representative of not only the army but the society, and government that ruled them. The flaws that damned William Judd Fetterman were celebrated in George Armstrong Custer, but destiny decreed that Fetterman's luck would run out nine and a half years before, and one hundred miles south, of Custer's.

The Plains Warriors didn't fight like the Confederates. Ostensibly it was guerilla warfare and not close order rank and file – small parties who would strike quickly and disengage. In battle there was no commander, nobody who issued orders. Each warrior fought his own battle for personal honour, for his family, his warrior society, clan,

Bull Elk

Whoever considers themselves beautiful,

after seeing me,

has no heart.

Lakota Elk Society Song

band and nation. Touching a live enemy, to 'count coup', was the bravest deed of all, far greater than mere killing. Invariably when opposing war parties clashed it was to defend hunting grounds, to avenge a transgression, or to gain honour against an hereditary foe. In most instances comparatively few casualties were sustained.

It was rare for such individualistic societies to

Behold The Foxes – Cub

amalgamate for an allied military campaign. 'Red Cloud's War' was one and the events surrounding June 1876 led to another. Red Cloud, like Sitting Bull ten years later, inspired unity by outlining a strategic agenda that through diplomacy and political prowess provided the motive, intent and objectives. His influence was great but not absolute, even amongst the Oglalas. Sitting Bull's nephew, White Bull, the Cheyenne Chiefs Little Wolf and Two Moons, Black Bear and Sorrell Horse from the Arapahos, the Sicangu Lakota Red Leaf, and Black Shield of the Mnikowojus, were all powerful voices on the Powder River. It was High Back Bone who planned Fetterman's demise and Crazy Horse who led the decoy party. Each recognised the days when counting coup was not enough.

Chiefs from the Crow Nation were among the first to touch the pen on the Treaty of 1868. When the ink had dried both Native American and Bluecoat warriors were still surprised that Red Cloud had attempted to persuade the Crow to join the Powder River alliance. The Crow military societies, the Foxes and Lumpwoods, had been willing, but the clan elders were reluctant to unite with their age old enemy, the Lakotas. They remained loyal to the United States, believing it to be their best chance of survival on a reservation of their choosing. 'Fathers, hear me. Call back your young men from the mountains of the bighorn sheep', implored Chief Bear Tooth at the Laramie Peace Commission, 'they have devastated the country and killed the elk, the deer, the antelope and my buffalo. They do not kill them to eat, they leave them to rot where they

fall. If I went into your country to kill your animals, what would you say?' The Crow made their choice knowing that the alternative was no choice at all.

The Bighorn Mountains and canyons are sacred to the Crow. Along the highways and hiking trails that traverse the area from Burgess Junction and Ten Sleep, there is still a chance to see those that Chief Bear Tooth sought to protect. All except the buffalo survive. Antelope abide in the lower elevations with black bears, shiras moose, beavers and racoons akin to the others who prefer the steep slopes and shade of Douglas-fir to the scraps of the desert basin. Sagebrush and Utah juniper comfort the canyon floors in the wake of the Bighorn River that has scythed through the plateau, leaving chunks of land severed and beached upon the prairie's shore. For some it is down there with the walleye, rainbow and brown trout, but for me it is in the mountains with those that the Crow's Creator, Old Man Coyote, placed upon this earth. It could have been here that a now extinct bird, similar to a blue-jay or magpie, inspired them to take the name 'Apsalooké', the 'Children Of The Large Beaked Bird', mistranslated as 'Crow' by the Europeans.

For as long as the Apsalooké have walked in them, these mountains and canyons have been bound to the bighorn sheep. They appear like centurions of the crags, their heads encased in coiled horns of armour over robes of dusk or tan. From October and deep into the moons of frost, the canyons resound with their battles, the rams clashing heads for the right to the ewes. Dignified then and always, they strut and stand imposing, the spread of their barrel magnificent yet carried with grace on a dancer's tip-toes. Equal to the buffalo, grizzly, wolf or elk, the bighorn sheep are as one with the American West. When all beneath the heights of Cloud Peak fell to the cartographer's invisible lines, the appetites and diseases of the bighorns' domestic descendants wiped them from these mountains.

Twilight Hunter – Lynx

Bighorn Rams

'Brothers look yonder! The boy clings to the pine tree as if it were his life. Save him!'
The bighorns made their way to the cliff ledge and bowed their heads.
'Take hold of our horns and we will save you.'
The rams pulled the boy from the edge and carried him to safety.
'Brothers, I honour you. I give this boy my name. I give him powers!'

Big Iron adopts a son – Apsalooké

The settlers' unbridled urge to shoot anything that moved accelerated the bighorn's demise but, paradoxically, the efforts and revenue of contemporary hunters contributes to the preservation of the four-leggeds and their domain. Nowadays the bighorn sheep have returned to Devil Canyon in the county that bears their name.

'White men with their "spotted buffalo" were on

Bear Cub

the plains about us. We made up our minds to be friendly to them', reflected Plenty Coups, the revered Crow Chief, 'their wise ones said we might have their religion but we found that there are too many kinds of religion among white men and scarcely any two agreed which was right to learn. This bothered us. These were not our ways. We kept the laws we made and lived our religion.' Essential to that religious belief is the sacred power transfigured in the Vision Quest. Guided by somebody who knows the holy path, purification in a sweat lodge and prayer precede the journey to a point that is raised to the heavens. There the body and mind must endure a fast, laying near naked and humble before the Powers, the two-leggeds, the four-leggeds, and the wings of the air, listening to their voices while awaiting the messenger's call. The vision seeker is advised to unite with the one who came to them by appealing to free their soul. Through that pledge they adopt the two-legged, the four-legged or the winged one's prowess and cherish their spiritual guidance. Personal medicine and images are inspired by the Vision Quest and honour the heart that came, and gave.

North of Highway 14 between Burgess Junction and the Bighorn River, a sacred Vision Quest and ceremonial site is laid bare at the summit of Medicine Mountain. The people the Crows called 'Bad Lodges', the Shoshones, and the Tsistsistas and Suhtais, were among the first to shelter in the Bighorns and breathe life into the Medicine Wheel. Even in these strange days of sending people and probes beyond the moon, this and other Medicine Wheels protect mysteries from the clutches of what some call progress. From a central stone cairn twenty-eight flared spokes reach out for six possible Vision Quest hollows. More conjecture than definition surrounds the Medicine Wheel. Do the spokes represent the days that elapse between the rising stars of Taurus, Orion and Canis Major? Did they serve as a calendar in relation to the stars, or to aid navigation across the plains? Is the significance of stellar alignments with the summer solstice related to the Sun Dance? Many keep asking.

It is conceivable that the Tsistsistas, who with the Suhtai became categorized as the Cheyenne, created the Medicine Wheel to represent the structure of the Wolf Lodge in the sacred earth giving ceremony, 'The Massaum', that united them as a people of distinct entity. The Cheyenne's Creator, Maheo, resided in the Wolf Lodge that, in the Medicine Wheel, might symbolize the centre of the universe. As spirit messengers, the two sacred wolves of the Massaum are guardians of the Cheyenne's holy mountain, Bear Butte, and all the four-leggeds on the surrounding prairie.

Fundamentally, the answer may be that the Old Ones have, if only for a moment, made us reconsider our relationship with the others who share this earth, and the promise above that seems distant but is displayed in stone before us. Look into the power of the circle and see the sun, the moon, the earth, the winds, your lifecycle and the rotation of the seasons. All are part of the Sacred Hoop of Life.

Striving to protect those sacred ways, the Cheyenne opposed the Shoshone who, like the Crow, elected for self-preservation and rode with the US Army on the good days to die. Forty miles northeast of Sheridan, concealed by bluffs from Montana Highway 314, Rosebud Creek is straddled by a gorge so lazy it has a permanent yawn on its lips. In the Centennial Summer of 1876, eight days before the Battle of the Little Bighorn, the Shoshone guided by Chief Washakie, and the Crow infused by Medicine Crow, confronted the Lakota and Cheyenne warriors of

Crazy Horse, Black Twin, Kicking Bear and Spotted Wolf, to save the command of Brigadier General George Crook. After the 'Battle of the Rosebud', Crook had to withdraw his column from the 'Sioux Campaign', leaving only two to converge on the Little Bighorn.

The Missouri River in North Dakota winds past the departure point of Custer's rendezvous on the Little Bighorn, before easing west into Knife River. The Hidatsa, 'The People Of The Willows', were cousins of the Crow and, along with the Mandan, they dominated the Knife River settlements. Knife River became a crucial trade centre, initially for Knife River flint but later for corn, blankets, horses, guns and the spoils of fur traders and trappers. The enterprise had grave consequences for the Shoshone who had been the equestrian lords of the plains through trading with their kin, the Comanche, but the Knife River network supplied their adversaries with both horses and guns. The Cree, Assiniboin, Lakota and, most vigorously of all, the Siksika, Blood and Piegan of the Blackfeet Confederacy, pressurised the Shoshone until they fell back to the Wind River region of Wyoming.

Meriwether Lewis and William Clark arrived on Knife River in the autumn of 1804. They stayed with the Hidatsas until the spring moons tempered the winter nights, leaving with the French trapper and interpreter, Toussaint Charbonneau, his Shoshone wife and infant son. The woman had been captured by the Hidatsas as a child and given the name Tsakaka-wias, 'Bird Woman'. She has been inaccurately consigned to the annals of Anglo-history as 'Sacajawea', a Shoshone term meaning 'canoe or boat launcher'.

Today the expedition route of Lewis and Clark is a designated National Historic Trail. Across Montana and Idaho alone there are thirty-one associated Lewis and Clark Historic Sites that, if they had voices, might sing hosanna for being placed in the midst of such immaculate conception. The zealous Virginians and their Corps of Discovery might have mumbled a chorus or two themselves on their deliverance from starvation by riders astride shining spotted horses. In the craving of hunger, the men on the Palouse Creek horses must have shimmered like ghosts, then angels.

The people were the Ne-Mee-Poo, 'The Real People', called Nez Perce by Canadian trappers, and the mounts that made such an impression on Lewis were Appaloosas, the breeding stock of the Nez Perce and their Plateau neighbours, the Palus and Cayuse. The Nez Perce tended to the explorers' needs, told them about the river route to the Pacific and helped them build canoes to take them there. Twisted Hair, Red Grizzly Bear, Broken Arm, Flint Necklace and the other headmen could not have imagined that in the ensuing years there wouldn't be enough canoes between the Cascades and Rocky Mountains for those who were determined to invade the 'Inland Empire'. Seventy-two years later the Nez Perce were hurrying up the same pass across the Bitteroot Mountains that Lewis and Clark had staggered down.

Grizzly Sow and Cub

Moose Cow and Calf

Highway 12 skirts the Lolo Trail. Before embarking upon the pass, the road spurs through East Kamiah, Idaho, where Coyote gave life to the Nez Perce when he slayed The Monster and clasped its heart until a trickle of blood settled upon the earth and merged with it to ignite their source. 'The earth is part of our body', the Nez Perce holy man Toohoolhoolzote instructed General O. O. Howard in May 1877, 'we came from the earth, and our bodies must go back to this earth, our Mother.' Despite all that he gave them, Coyote could not quell the prospectors' lust for gold. Reneging on guarantees to the contrary, the US Government issued a proclamation opening the Wallowa Valley to white settlement when gold was discovered and, as a consequence of their forced removal, the Nez Perce out fought and out thought the US Army in a fourteen hundred mile pursuit of sanctuary between June and October 1877. Looking Glass, the grandson of Flint Necklace, guided the warriors with Lean Elk and Ollokot, each believing in the strength of their 'Wyakin', their spiritual guardian from the four-leggeds or wings of the air.

Even though he was a Civil Chief and not a war leader, it is Ollokot's brother, Thunder Travelling To Loftier Mountain Heights, who will forever be associated with the courage of the Nez Perce. Their father, Tuekakas, had once converted to Christianity and received the name 'Joseph', after which the Americans called Thunder Travelling To Loftier Mountain Heights, 'Young Joseph', and later, Chief Joseph. On 5 October 1877, forty-two miles from the Canadian border and the safety they sought with Sitting Bull and his Lakota refugees, Chief Joseph delivered the Nez Perce's surrender to the overwhelming US forces of Howard and Miles at the base of the Bear's Paw Mountains in Montana.

They may have dumped his body in a pauper's grave but no-one can separate Sitting Bull's soul from the heart of this land. His greatest demonstration of unity with all that connects the sacred hoop came in Montana during the Sun Dance before the Battle of the Little Bighorn. Sitting Bull had dreamt of the Deer Medicine Rocks, where the ancient ones had left their marks and the Powers carved their own. With the sacred rocks as his witness, Sitting Bull gave of himself so that the people would live, and in his vow came a vision of soldiers falling that foretold of a battle and victory.

If you didn't know to look, you would probably drive past the clique of sandstones sprouting from the shallow red crested bowl, north of Lame Deer, without a second glance. They loom old and a little cantankerous, peeved at being so exposed. They may be silent, but apprehension and mystery hum a seductive chant, and as you walk towards them through the dust boiling from the guttered track, you imagine them blinking in the sun, blinking in the rain and blinking in the yellow wind that shifts at and around them from the ground. Their pointed hats and smooth bald heads stoop against the dirty Sunday sky, the flagging sun hardly bothering to twitch across Rosebud

Trumpeter Swans

Black Bear

Creek and the valley. One crouched, two standing, the creek watcher leaning, all four are hunched together from one side. Edge around the verge and the four become eight, still reluctant to attest for a stranger. No Johnny-come-lately smile and nod will work for you here, not even the one where you give the waitress the eye and she smiles back, as the home town diners let the last gulp of coffee swill between their cheeks until they've scrutinized and are satisfied that you're not worth the trouble of letting their eggs go cold. There is nothing that the Deer Medicine Rocks want to tell an imposter, though they tolerate the intrusion. It's tempting to touch just because you can but you glance over your shoulder first, then hesitate again at the scuffling of swallow

Bear's Lodge

chicks in the knotted terrace of nests. Elk, turtles, bighorns, grizzly bears and deer, warriors, holy men, promises and prayers, soldiers without ears falling like grasshoppers upside down, are all etched here.

It wasn't the hands of men but the claws of bears that gouged each rigid stripe into the sentinel of the Belle Fourche River. Explanations differ as to how this obelisk of rock came to dominate the Missouri Buttes around Hulett, Wyoming. In the years since Colonel Richard I. Dodge was duped into naming it 'Devil's Tower', geologists have described the temple of igneous rock as the neck of an extinct volcano that gained its mantle of sheer grooves and elephantine hide from the sedate cooling of magma that contracted and ribbed the waking giant beneath a sedimentary veneer. Long before it was painted as a pillar for conquest, the people who respected its spirit of conception told how a group of boys had once left camp to challenge each other's boasts. Unwittingly, they provoked a colossal grizzly bear and realising that their weapons were useless, one of them placed a sacred stone on the ground and called the others to gather around him. As the bear advanced they began their braveheart songs and prayed

to the powers within the One above. Suddenly the stone dilated and they stepped upon it. With the bear's first swipe, the stone extended skyward and when the grizzly saw the futility of his efforts he left them on top of the column of rock that his anger had helped to create.

The Lakota recount the intervention of Fallen Star, a guardian and messenger between this and the other world, who answered the pleas of a brother and sister by commanding the earth to rise and lift them from the grasp of a furious bear clan who, like the solitary grizzly, clawed in vain at the rock. From then, Mato tipi la paha, The Hill of the Bear's Lodge, stood inside the Sacred Circle of the Black Hills. The Lakota followed the sun's path on earth in the Spring Ceremonial Journey, converging upon the Bear's Lodge for the Sun Dance when, with the arrival of the summer solstice, it became the Gray Buffalo Horn. The journey began with the Pipe Ceremony on the first day of spring, a prayer for the renewal of life on earth and the return of the four-leggeds and wings of the air. Then as now, when the sun enters the Bear's Lodge it provides the spark that ignites the pipe.

There aren't any 'devils' here, only the spirit of the bear that dwells within. When you hear the growl deep inside, it is impossible to ignore. The day before I listened at the Bear's Lodge, I had seen a grizzly bear clambering up a hillside behind the old hunting camp of Buffalo Bill Cody. The grizzly monopolized my thoughts and at the Bear's Lodge it became clear that I had to turn back to Pahaska. The night was a long time passing there, in one of Cody's draughty cabins. The frosted window and garnish of ice in the washroom wasn't inviting but I fumbled and guessed in the seamless pitch in an attempt to reduce my scent. The parts of the door that were acquainted with the frame sighed as a bevy of frigid air pushed past as I closed it behind me and started for the shred of sapphire simmering

Moose

Honour Manitou. Take only what He grants.
Nanabush, son of Mortal Woman and the West Wind,
go with my grandson, Tooth, to the moose in the valley.
Respect the moose, he gives his life so you may live.
I say again, take only what you need. Manitou is watching . . .

She Wolf's Warning – Ojibwa

At the trailhead – Grizzly Bear

around the steeples of pine in the east of the Wapiti Valley. The sky became ripe, all peaches and cream, but I still couldn't see what the river was babbling about until every rock and bush and upended stump suddenly looked like a bear. Every time I yawned or my stomach rattled I reminded myself that they were here. With the sun heaving itself toward the centre, it was a good time to move on and ignore the distractions.

My footsteps whispered *shh, shh, shh, shh* in the last smattering of snow until the next, as I walked into a wind that pretended to be timid but in its chill was the swan-song of winter. Even without seeing them, they had brought me from the madness and helped me to remember what they had never forgotten in the fire of green and blue and grey and white. I waited a long time. It must have been ten hours. It didn't matter. It was an eagle's cry that pealed over the tendrils dragging behind the boats of cloud. There weren't any signs. No tiara of points on front foot tracks or pointed heels to the back. No traumatised earth, shrubs or trees in recoil from sharp-set two inch claws. No respite from meagre days laying still beneath a ragged shroud. In grizzly country a motionless bundle covered with twigs and grass has one possessive owner and only a fool would loiter if the concealed carcass wasn't theirs. Ignorance isn't bliss out here.

At the trailhead I stopped and gave thanks for this day. I wanted it to last for ever. A grudging braid of dust floating aimlessly above the ridge at my side provided an excuse to linger. The shelf was squat, not more than two hands above my head. I knew it was getting late when I thought I saw a shock of auburn hair nudging into the cloud. I knew I had to take a deep breath when the shock became a hump that instinctively snapped back. Through the intensity of the grizzly's expression there was a vulnerability I hadn't expected. His eyes were curious with a width of alarm, almost lost in a sundown face. Teetering slightly like a burly man wearing new stack heeled boots, he straightened his back to peer down at me from the ledge. It wasn't fear but remorse that was disconcerting as he toddled forward on two legs. How do you face a woman if you've killed her man, or the man if you've taken his brother, or the child left alone by either? I couldn't answer. With a flurry of dirt, snorts and fur, he hit the ground in a heap of ripples that splashed up and down his body as he bounded forward and stuck to the edge. He fixed on me again and I couldn't let go. His nostrils flared as he blew and grumbled, a delicate

Mountain Goat

thread of saliva trickling from his bottom lip. Attached to his stare, I looked out, he looked in and we wondered. His hair flattened and my heart dropped out of my throat. Somewhere between irritated and uneasy he decided that I wasn't a threat and I understood that he didn't want to be disturbed. He dipped out of sight then shuffled down the slope towards me before he stopped and asked again. As he walked away from the trailhead I thanked him for this day.

Entering bear country, particularly grizzly habitat, without any knowledge of bear behaviour is only advisable if you can run at over 30mph or you find the prospect of standing stock still and waving your arms above your head an attractive one as 600lb of aggrieved grizzly bounces towards you. The bear might be bluffing, but if it's not, the only option is to roll into a ball face down on the floor, protecting your internal organs. Bears are not killers but tragedies do occur. A grizzly sow with cubs has few equals when it comes to demanding respect, only a moose cow with a calf shares a similarly irascible reputation. With luck both might be encountered off highway 14-16-20 between Cody and the east entrance to Yellowstone, on the North Fork of the Shoshone River.

Whenever I drive down that road my mind skips back to growing pains and school days. Nobody wanted to be the awkward kid in class with bones that appeared to have outgrown their skin. I remember that self-conscious loner who hid in the background and was always the butt of jokes. They were never described as tall or elegant, but gangly, lanky or clumsy. When I see a young rawboned moose stumble across the highway I think of that awkward kid, but anybody who has trudged ankle deep through marsh and been trapped by a web of willows will testify that a moose has grace. Their silhouettes materialize when the day begins or ends, standing solitary and brooding like serenity's first born. Unmistakable, not ungainly, gaping tines flare from the palmate hammocks slung over the bulls' bursting summer brows, their lean shanks flicked with wisps of silver

Old Faithful

and their bodies glowing rich and chestnut brown. Taller than a man at the peak of prominent withers, they high step and guzzle then in the shadows melt away. The strapping figure of the bull moose, and the cow's belligerence under threat, are sufficient to curb most appetites. With the exception of vehicles and seasonal guns, only grizzly bears, mountain lions and wolves make the West wild for moose.

Wolves have been restored to the steaming child of lava and ice that seethes and hisses and with stealth bewitches. Described by the Hidatsa as Rock Yellow Water, 'Mi-tsi-a-da-zi', or Yellowstone – it doesn't matter what it's called because its spirit will never leave you. Cloaked by the whiff of sulphur churning from a thermal cauldron, I bowed to the impatient darkness and crouched in the straggling light to witness two brothers venture to the river before it vanished into the night. Anytime you see a wolf is like the first. One was dusky, the other bright, animated with the joy of freedom and what it is to be alive. It is easy to understand why the Lakotas and Cheyennes called their scouts 'wolves', and to relate to the Cheyenne message that it was the wolf who taught them how to hunt. Just as the wolf sings to the raven, coyote and fox, the Cheyenne call the wolf to their harvest.

This pair reminded me of Glooskap and Malsum, the wolf twins of Algonquian lore. Glooskap created the sun and moon, the two-leggeds, the four-leggeds, the winged, and those who live in the waters, leaving Malsum to engender the mountains and valleys. In the Teton Range and Jackson Hole Valley there can be nothing but forgiveness for Malsum's malevolent spirit. Sucked abruptly from the earth without warning, the Tetons are the pleasure that follows the pain. Their beautiful violence bristles blue-slate and grey to contradict the passive Snake River. Before John Colter crossed this valley, and William Sublette named it for his partner, David Jackson, the Bannock Shoshones, 'the Sheep Eaters', risked their lives to stay. When you enter this glorious valley ask yourself who wouldn't do the same.

Wolf I Am

In darkness, in light,

wherever I search, wherever I run, wherever I stand,

everything will be good,

because Maheo protects us.

Cheyenne Scout Song

Lynx

It sounds like a love song. In the morning when the cool air slaps your face to wake you and later, much later, when the bitten or shallow or rotund moons disregard their inhibitions and sit in naked glory, the chorus of bleeding hearts goes on until the tune is as dry and wasted as ashes, blowing from an abandoned fire hole. But even wavering and hoarse, the empty spaces and memories that are lost and found between the mountains cry 'If this is love, then love is war'. The call to arms of the brindle royals, imperials and monarchs, sets a chorus line of follies loose to cavort up and down the human spine. Has there ever been a more honest expression of emotion than the bull elk's ballad of autumn pain?

The challenges of lust and passion are wailed in the midst of highland timber from the Northern Rockies, through Yellowstone and San Juan, to the mountains of New Mexico. Behind groves of rusting aspen that whisper like skinny white girls with peroxide perms, a glissando ascending through alto and soprano pipes up to a shriek then shatters in a trine of gasping King Kong coughs. The cows watch their champion go and await the retreat of the loser with a

settlers in eager pursuit. Little Wolf belonged to one of the Cheyenne's most respected warrior societies, The Elks, and in common with his brothers-in-arms, he had been imbued through vision and admiration with the qualities of a valiant bull elk. Such reverance can be chased over a span of eleven thousand years. Earth mounds sculptured into bull elk on the Winnebago's ancestral lands in Wisconsin pre-date the Hopewellian civilizations of AD 500 by two thousand years and, along the Cumberland River in Tennessee, the Shawnee were the first to call the elk 'wapiti'. The bull's indomitable will, strength and virility, inspiring appearance and implacable defence of a susceptible gang remain attributes worthy of honouring with spirit. Through ceremony and devotion, Lakota Elk Dreamers and Society members amalgamate with the elk in soul. The spirit tracks left by the four-legged confirm their brotherhood, a connection in the sacred hoop that is painted with a rainbow.

The rainbow spans the 'Powers of the West' and blazes a trail for each of the Thunder Beings. In western Colorado, when the first thunder of spring wakes the bear from

ON THE TRAIL OF THE RIO GRANDE

combination of grace and aloof disdain. Parading antlers sprawling high and wide, and bulging eyes rolling red with pride, the victor returns to his hareem of spoils to vaunt the prowess exploding within his tawny cloak and dark brown hood that is pumped with adrenalin and muscle and blood.

Harbouring a larger population of elk than any other state, Colorado provides a well trodden stage for the rut's annual dramatics. During the bull elk's wild recitals of 1878, Little Wolf brushed Colorado's eastern border with Dull Knife and two hundred and ninety-seven Cheyennes in a harrowing flight for survival. With fewer than one hundred warriors in their number, they risked a fifteen hundred mile exodus from 'Indian Territory' in Oklahoma, to their Suhtai homelands around the Yellowstone, with 'winter kill', ten thousand soldiers and three thousand souvenir hungry

hibernation, the Utes celebrate the earth's regeneration with the 'Bear Dance'. When only the 'Ones Who Speak Clearly' rode beyond the red rock rim of the Colorado Plateau, south to the Animas River, a warrior returning from a spring hunt found a bear still fast in winter's sleep. He touched the bear and sang how the snows had gone, waiting for the sunlight to persuade the bear's eyes. The bear awoke and thanked the warrior by teaching him a dance to share with his people that, each time the world became new, would unite them with all life on, above and below the earth.

Imitating a bear when the sun entices then splits a den's gloom, the dancers shillyshally into the brushwood arbour with laboured movements and squinting eyes, their faces creased with feigned sleep and the cheek of daylight's surprise. The two lines of bodies sway with the hint that both

Bugling Elk

are stirring to the drums and voices which slowly rouse, but though face to face and close at arms length, for the women to reach the men takes more than dance steps. The hunger, she knows, gives her freedom to choose who she will lead to the warmth that enlivens the bear's appetite.

The people of the Seven Ute Nations; the Mouache, Capote, Weeminuche, Uncompahgre, Uintah, Yampa and Parianuc can hear the earth's heartbeat through the rock of Uncompahgre Peak, and for centuries they ensured that the pulse retained a contented hum by bartering for horses with the Spanish in mid-seventeenth century Santa Fe, and guiding traders along the 'Old Spanish Trail' that trickled over corners of their sacred 'Shining Mountains' to the Spaniard's 'City of Angels'. But others came who sought different ways, and what they found in the mountains made them stay. The Utes who watched were overwhelmed by the sight of a Bluecoat army trooping on Santa Fe, and then relentless hordes of singing 'Forty-niners' who jettisoned 'Oh Susanna' for 'California' along the way. And even in the Shining Mountains, the miners and settlers aboard covered prairie schooners, and Bluecoats and Blackrobes still came.

Captain John Gunnison entered the Ute's domain in September 1853 to charter a passage for the transcontinental railroad, but he bypassed the canyon that now bears his name. Still the best kept secret in the West; fifteen miles east of present day Montrose, Colorado, the world plummets and ascends in a jumble of marbled veins that wriggle through a posse of box-elders and away from the river's dash, to the pillars and posts of each ragged wall, and the shadows cast from gamble oak and juniper's twines. The Utes kept the Black Canyon's secret until the Hayden Geological Expedition of 1873/74.

A party of Uncompahgres tracked Gunnison's column in the Black Canyon region as he crossed the Ute trails that provided the basis for the area's contemporary roads. Highway 550 runs from Montrose to Durango, past Uncompahgre Peak, and on south of the San Juan Mountains. If you placed your ear to the Ute's peak today, the earth's heartbeat would probably be muffled by the 'Durango & Silverton' steam train stuttering along the line like a toothless preacher leading a faithful congregation to the Promised Land. I've never seen Canaan or the River Jordan, but I wish I had if it surpasses all of this which is so blessed.

Freedom to choose – Black Bear

The San Juan Mountains portray old fashioned brides on their wedding days, all laced in white and coy and twinkling in pristine pool eyes, that flutter aside meadows lit by posies waiting prim and china dainty. You can't see the end of innocence but knowing is enough. At Conejos, Chief Ouray and nine other Ute leaders signed a treaty that secured all Ute lands in Colorado west of the Continental Divide, but part of the bargain was relinquishing what fanned across the east, and the mineral rights for their entire reservation. One beneficiary was Frederick Pitkin, a future State Governor, who became rich on the back of San Juan silver. Propped up by his new found fortune, Pitkin advocated annexing the San Juan Mountains from the Ute's reservation. On 13 September 1873, Ouray signed the 'agreement' that ceded the entire San Juan region.

Like so many Western figures, Ouray remains tangled in contradictions, and under this boundless sky that bends to kiss the brides, his detractors find the contention. A provision of the 1873 treaty accorded Ouray a 'salary' of $1,000 annually for ten years, a house and one hundred and sixty acres of land. But if he did succumb to human frailty it was probably for love, not money. His only son, Paron, had been captured by some Lakotas during a skirmish over hunting rights. The boy was only five years old at the time and the government became aware of Ouray's desperation. The treaty negotiator, Felix Brunot, promised Ouray that if he assisted the government, it would employ its influence to secure his son's release.

Traitor or saviour of his people, Ouray looks down from the rotunda of Colorado's state capital building alongside fifteen other 'pioneers', each immortalized in stained glass as the 'Founding Fathers of Colorado'. It seems a long way from the 'Meeker Uprising' and Governor Pitkin's 'The Utes Must Go!' propaganda campaign. In terms of Native American representation, only the face of Colorado's contemporary US Senator, Ben Nighthorse Campbell, can have become as familiar as Ouray's in Denver's corridors of power.

Denver appears to grow by the hour, moving ever closer to all of the other cities that look like nowhere in particular but virtually the same as the last one you got lost in. The criss-cross network of four to eight lanes, to where-the-hell-did-he-come-from highways, obliterate any thoughts of rutted gullies, dirt lashed canvas and bare lumber held together by tall tales from small men knee deep in spit and mud. D. C. Oakes, an Iowa based writer, was one of those

men who through his books and yarns about gold strikes incited the Pike's Peak Gold Rush that closed the 1850s and opened Denver City.

If the San Juan Mountains are the brides, in southeastern Colorado a thousand bridesmaids linger in dowdy patchwork pinafores of faded greens and yellows that flop from here and now to wherever and then on past nothing at all. East of Pueblo, where Highway 50 is absorbed by 194, the town of La Junta nestles in a bend of the Arkansas River that begins its arc beside Bent's Old Fort. Sixty years after their grandfather, Silas Bent, had instigated the Boston Tea Party, Charles and William Bent went into business with Ceran St Vrain and established a Western legacy. The reconstructed adobe walls and bastions of Bent's Old Fort that blush against the flagging backdrop are faithful to the originals of 1833 which once housed Kit Carson, Jim 'Medicine Calf' Beckwourth and Thomas 'Brokenhand' Fitzpatrick as sometimes Bent's Fort employees. The Bluecoats who made such an impression on the Utes, 'The Army of The West', marched on Santa Fe from here and, upon taking the city, General Steven Watts Kearny installed Charles Bent as the first American Governor of New Mexico on 22 September 1846, but Charles' tenure, and life, ended four months later during the Taos rebellion.

William Bent continued to develop a favourable reputation with individuals and bands from the Plains Nations and was appointed 'Indian Agent' by the government. The Cheyenne Chief, Yellow Wolf, had originally advised him where to locate the fort, and his marriage to Owl Woman, and subsequent family, consummated his position among the Cheyennes. In 1859, Bent reported that, in his region, 'the Cheyennes and Arapahos scrupulously maintain peaceful relations with the whites', as one hundred and fifty thousand settlers floated up the Platte, Arkansas and Republican Rivers, and rolled over ancestral buffalo ranges, on their pilgrimage to Pike's Peak. Attempting to secure 'peaceful relations', one of the Arapaho's Chiefs, Little Raven, visited Denver City and 'pledged his word for peace', but his expression, and that of most who followed, became strained when the Treaty of Fort Wise left them destitute in their own country.

Colorado's Territorial Governor, John Evans, was running for Senator, and his military commander, Colonel John Chivington, for Congress, and both identified the resolution to Colorado's 'Indian problem' as crucial to their campaigns. By the spring of 1864 Chivington was insisting that *all* Native Americans, including women, children, and new born babies, should be exterminated because 'Nits make lice', issuing orders to 'Kill Cheyennes wherever found'. His favourite officers, Eayre, Dunn and Downing, responded enthusiastically, as their commands attacked, burned, looted and murdered Cheyenne and Arapaho men, women and children into the summer of '64.

On 11 June, four Arapaho wanderers unwittingly provided them with an opportunity to rally further support, when they were disturbed by a ranch-hand's wife during a fraught attempt to run off a herd of thirty horses. The woman and her two children screamed frantically and from the psyche of plains survival, where it was taught from birth that one imprudent cry could alert an enemy and call disaster, one of the men lost his nerve in the confusion of shrieks, neighs, squeals and closing gunshots. The woman and her children were muffled by death, and when he arrived, her husband joined them. The bodies of the Hungate family were taken to Denver and placed on public display. With the city locked in frenzy, Evans sought authority to raise a one hundred day militia of 'Indian Fighters' to supplement Chivington's forces. So began another cycle of violence that culminated northeast of Bent's Old Fort, above present day Brandon, along a dry wash called Sand Creek.

When the first light of 29 November 1864, seeped over the plains and blinked above the distant sand hills, a Cheyenne woman tending her cooking fire became distracted by the rumble of hooves. Peering into the lank winter dawn she noticed a dust cloud rising with the sound, and popped back inside her lodge to announce that a herd of buffaloes were approaching. Today the only dust and rumble advancing on Sand Creek comes from the occasional vehicle crunching up the rigid dirt road that pokes through the surrounding crops. A conspicuous red sign requests that you 'STOP!' before entering, and crossing the creek. It would be easy to ignore it, there is nobody around to say that you did. But if you did, it would be *knowing* that you had. It's worth stuffing a couple of dollars in the expectant tin to ease morality's pinch. An ugly stone marker set knee high on a block of concrete meets you, 'Sand Creek Battle Ground. Nov. 29 & 30 1864'. Well, at least the mason managed to get the location and date right.

The land matches the headstone, the scrub barely softened by a curl of cottonwood and willow. Oblivious, the foliage lines the dry creek bed but does nothing to ease the horrible silence. This is one of those places you want to run away from but in your mind it always follows. As hardened as we are to cameras gobbling up blood-spattered pictures and disgorging the tragedy into our homes, I find it impossible to comprehend the barbarous depravity that left this dour scrap of land looking like an abattoir. 'Well, I long to be wading in gore', Chivington had guffawed to his officers in the hours leading up to the attack, and when they disengaged the dismembered bodies of one hundred and five Cheyenne and Arapaho women and children were strewn where I was about to place my feet. Of the thirty-five men who were able to defend the helpless, twenty-eight fell at their sides. And though I look and will always remember, I don't want to walk where any of them died.

No doubt the image of Chief Black Kettle gripping the United States flag and calling for the women and children to gather around him would have made the front pages and opening titles of CNN. The flag was a gift from Abraham Lincoln with a promise that if he flew it above his camp for all to see, every soldier would STOP! And never attack. 'Black Kettle raised the American flag and a white flag', testified Agent Colley, 'they retreated up the creek. They were followed up and pursued and killed and butchered. They were cut to pieces in almost every manner and form.' Captain Silas Soule, and Lieutenants Cramer and Connor, had opposed the attack, enraging Chivington who stormed 'Damn any man who sympathizes with Indians! I have come to kill Indians and believe it right and honorable to use any means under God's heaven to kill Indians.' Soule ordered his men to hold their fire and abstain from mutilating the dead or dying. 'It looked too hard for me', he wrote, 'to see little children on their knees begging for their lives and having their brains beaten out like dogs.' It is hard to imagine worse, but there was.

Congress condemned Chivington and his accomplices but although investigated, none were ever tried. The Ohio born Methodist Preacher and Sunday School teacher spent the rest of his life fabricating and defending his actions, and those of the six hundred under his command. Silas Soule volunteered to testify against Chivington and became the victim of Colorado's first political assassination. 'All we ask is that we may have peace with the whites . . . I want all these Chiefs of the soldiers here to understand that we are for peace, and that we may not be mistaken for enemies', Black Kettle had impressed upon Colonel Chivington and Governor Evans at the Camp Weld Peace Conference two months before the massacre. Governor Evans prospered politically and financially. Chief Black Kettle survived Sand Creek but four years later was trampled beneath the hooves of Custer's Seventh Cavalry, whose attack on the Cheyenne's

Navajo Moon

peaceful village along the Washita was reminiscent of Chivington's . . . I drive away from Sand Creek and damn the butchers who made the horrible silence.

Wandering southwest, the trail fords the romance of the Rio Grande where the dreams of dreamers and loners become horses surging at a gallop with their manes and tails billowing like the spray bursting from the river when all that matters, and ever did before, was crossing this and any of those Godforsaken borders that have stopped you reaching old Mexico. Viva outlaws and gamblers and bandits in white hats, and to hell with it for a while. And for a while there will be some kind of freedom. But it doesn't last. Sooner or later there will be hell to pay.

Dusk side of the Rio Grande, with head bowed, another Sand Creek kneels between the Galiuro and Pinaleno Mountains in Aravaipa Canyon. 'A memorable and glorious morning', is how Jesus Elias, a leader of the Tucson Ring's Mexican, American and Papago mob described 30 April 1871. The one hundred and forty-four women and children slaughtered at Camp Grant by William S. Oury's outlaws and gamblers and bandits belonged to a Western Apache division of Arivaipa. 'When I made peace with Lieutenant Whitman my heart was very big and happy', rued Eskiminzin, the Arivaipa headman, 'the Tucson people write for their papers and tell their own story. The Apaches have no one to tell their story.'

Searching for the mythical province of Cíbola in 1540,

Francisco Vásquez de Coronado commented upon a body of people inhabiting the Southern Plains whom, it was assumed, were 'Athapaskans of some sort', the linguistic relations of peoples who ranged far to the frozen north. The Zuñi referred to the 'newcomers' as 'apachu', 'the enemy', which the Spaniards merged with the Tewa Pueblo term 'Navahuu', to form 'Apaches de Nabaju', before the Southern Athapaskans were recognised as 'Apache' and 'Navajo'. The Navajo adopted both Pueblo and Spanish influences into their culture but for every horse, sheep, cow, fruit tree or iron tool the Pueblos first acquired, the conquistadors exacted a brutal toll. The Seven Cities of silver and gold Coronado craved for were, in reality, fashioned from adobe and stone. His castle in the air lost, Coronado began to subjugate those he found.

The Hopi, the Zuñi, and the eighteen Rio Grande Pueblo units tolerated the pain and have preserved their heritage with dignity. In museums and on library shelves some may be San Juan, San Felipe, Santa Ana, Santa Clara or San Ildefonso, but their blood remains Ohkay, Katishtya, Tamaja, Kha P'o, and Po-woh Ge-Oweenge. In a lifeway devoted to community, family and spiritual harmony, each individual has a responsibility to maintain the delicate balance between the two-leggeds, the four-leggeds and the winged. All is animate and interrelated within Pueblo theocracies.

Stacked on wind scoured mesas, each home seems to have been delivered, but not built, by human hands, pulled from the earth as it strained in labour to push sets of pueblo quadruplets through the desert floor. The interdependence of each smooth cubic dwelling declares the communality of those within, providing steps from the ceilings of clay and meaning to other worlds, unscathed by time. Protected inside the walls of the sacred Kiva, the Sipapuni in the base of the ceremonial chamber represents the opening out of

Western Diamondback Rattlesnake

'Choose the gray rattler'. Stroke it gently with a feather.
Tell the chief 'this is the one who will be my wife',
Spider Grandmother instructed the boy from Tokonave.
The snake girl removed her skin and stood before him – a beautiful young woman,
who forever reminded him of the knowledge imparted by the Snake People –
the ceremonies and songs that bring the rain.

Origin of The Snake Clan and Dance – Hopi

which the Pueblos emerged into this, the Upper World.

Basking in the shifting moods of sun and season, the rocky dunes rippling yonder that wait to catch the sky should it eventually decide to fall, were the first to see the Hopi clamber upon the Fourth World. At the confluence of the Colorado and Little Colorado Rivers in the Grand Canyon, some Hopis identify a gurgling leonine

Betatakin

spring oozing ochre tinged water as the Sipapuni of mankind. When there was only Tokpella, the Endless Space, Tawa created the First World, after which His messenger, Spider Grandmother, guided the 'Chosen People' who followed Tawa's 'Road of Life', above the spiritual desolation that had wrecked the previous worlds. As they entered the Fourth World, Yawpa, the mockingbird, assigned each to a race and nation, and gave them a direction to take in the impending migrations. After four days all were to leave the Sipapuni, but before departing each was to choose an ear of corn from Yawpa's array. The Hopis deliberated until only a stunted blue cob remained. 'Your lives will be full of toil and hardship', Yawpa told them, 'but your years will be many.' Different groups followed separate stars and developed clans that reflected their experiences. The antelope, snake, coyote and bear honoured their clan members by offering their skins, so they and the Hopi would become one when both shared the same robe.

The Bear Clan were the first to reach the place where the blue corn grows and settled at Oraibi, possibly the oldest continually inhabited settlement in the United States. 'I have washed away the footprints of your Emergence', the Creator's nephew, Sotuknang, reminded the Hopis, 'but the day will come if you preserve the memory and meaning of your Emergence, when those stepping stones will appear again to prove the truth you speak.' For many Hopis, those stepping stones are seen in Fremont petroglyphs, and found in Anasazi 'cliff palaces'

and Sinagua villages, pre-dating AD 500. Scattered across the southwest and Four Corners region; Wupatki, Mesa Verde, Chaco Canyon, Betatakin and Keet Steel exemplify the 'Old Ones' of the Hopi, Zuñi, and Rio Grande Pueblos.

The San Francisco Peaks that dominate present day Flagstaff, Arizona, were among the Fourth World's first creations and residing above, in the 'cloud house' of Neuvatikyao, are the Kachinas. As deities from the other worlds, the Kachinas bring power and wisdom to the Hopi 'Road of Life' by teaching the harmony and balance, good over evil, that gives life and spirit to all things. In sacred ceremonies, the Kachinas provide physical expression to the Creator's plan. In tourist traps and 'trading post' windows, the carved dolls depicting Kachina spirits are bought and sold as vacation mementos, but nobody can buy what only the Hopi know.

Perspective wraps the San Francisco Peaks in the shimmering threads weaved into the Painted Desert. The [Navajo] Diné call the pastel furrows 'halchíítah', 'amidst the colours', and look beyond the shore of the Little Colorado's extravagant beach to Dook'o'ooslííd (the San Franciscos), the western fringe of Diné Bikéyah, their sacred homeland. First Man and First Woman ushered the Diné into the World of Light near Dibé Nitsaa, the northern peak of Diné Bikéyah in the La Plata range of the San Juan Mountains.

The mountain boundaries of the south and east, Dsoodzil (Mt Taylor, NM) and Sis Najiní (Mt Blanca, Co), were breached in 1863/64 when Kit Carson conducted a force of New Mexican and Californian Civil War hopefuls to 'ethnically cleanse' the Diné from their sacred lands. Carson killed everything to which the Diné gave life, concluding his carnage by defiling the serenity of the Canyon de Chelly, before the Diné surrendered and were forced to suffer the 'Long Walk' to General James Carleton's Bosque Redondo concentration camp.

Malnutrition, disease and exposure claimed hundreds who had avoided army bullets, but the Diné held on to their belief in life, and after signing the Treaty of 1868 they walked back with the songs of the Blessing Way, entering the hogan of the Four Mountains, blessed at each corner by the women of Water, Corn, Mountain and Earth.

Coyote

Whether the Diné and N'dé entered the southwest down one or both sides of the Rocky Mountains, or as told in the spoken word, the exact dates and passing years crumble in the wake of human experience. How, and whenever it was, so much of what we have become struggles to relate to the challenges they defied. But, assuming they walked this way, we *can* share with them and believe that, somewhere within us, our first impressions were once theirs in this land so bloodied with embers and haunted by figures cut from burning stone.

Twisting through Utah's Arches and Canyonlands National Parks, we can see what they saw, lay our hands where they touched and laud the creation of Delicate Arch and all the glittering beds of red rock nails. According to ancient Paiute lore, the 'standing rocks' of Bryce Canyon were once the two-legged and four-legged Legend People who Coyote turned to stone for deceiving the Creator. If the Paiutes' descendants felt threatened or intrigued by the strangers slinking through their candy store of orange rock en route to Sonora may, like so much, only be known by the ravens who now, as then, idly roll on the thermals that lounge below the long blue keeper of secrets.

Sun-up, sundown or crippling 'High Noon', each tall Sonoran recluse waits with arms expectant for that once in a lifetime day when so near will not be so far. Presenting pure white blooms that are soon agape with pollen splattered like egg yolk on dinner plates, they endure the rejection their invitation guarantees but hold onto the flowers until the morning after. Way out of reach, the stands of saguaro cactus stretching above forty feet have been 'stood up' every May and June for the past hundred and some years, forsaken each time by reluctant 'darlings'.

'Buenos días. I always say that to strangers. Makes 'em feel like ol' times. Need a drink? Or something.' Tequila or whisky? It was such a tough decision, I managed to splutter 'coffee'. Black, of course . . . 'Alrighty', she said, trying to restrain her eyebrows. Her dress was a little too short and frilly, the waistband a little too tight and her shirt open one button too many. But her face remembered what it was like to be pretty beneath the layers of make-up caked old and new and one for good luck. As she poured I listened to so much big talk, out of big beards, below big hats, with big bellies obscuring big buckles, that I thought I'd died and gone to Texas. She slid the coffee along the bar and followed it, propping herself on folded arms so I could see that the extra button wasn't open but missing. 'You stayin' in Tucson or here in Tombstone?' The sparkle in her eye matching the beads of sweat and grease twinkling on her forehead and nose. Maybe this was my chance to be Doc Holliday. She kept asking and I kept smiling and nodding to stop my face creasing at the coffee that could have stripped the boardwalk, but she was no 'soiled dove' or 'calico queen'. Her husband rode bulls for a living, and I never wanted to be Doc anyway, so I joined a Gila woodpecker and a red tailed hawk, in accepting the shade and company of the nearest saguaro. There, in the haze of 'Old West' clichés, I could almost see them, bolting around the cactus staked desert on paint horses, chasing after Bluecoats and stagecoaches. In southern Arizona you *sure can* buy any image that has ever been peddled.

Although they learnt to live with the Sonoran desert and the clanking chimes of San Xavier and every other mission bell, the truth of the various peoples categorised as 'Apache', was born in the mountains. When the earth was new, Usen, the One God and Giver of Life, warned another who was pure in spirit and heart, that a great flood would engulf the earth. Usen instructed Changing Woman to search for a large abalone shell, and when the waters eventually receded, the shell beached her upon White Sands, in what is now New Mexico. Walking alone, Changing Woman longed for children and with Usen's intervention she conceived a child by the sun, and gave birth to Killer of Enemies. Then, from the touch of water, her second son was Child of the Water. The boys devoted their lives to the N'dé, The [Apache] People. Child of the Water slayed the Giant who had terrorized The People since the first moon, and Killer of Enemies liberated the four-leggeds from the darkness of the world below.

It was Usen's wish that The People live in harmony with the earth, the two-leggeds, the four-leggeds, the winged, and those who swim in the waters, so He sent the Mountain Spirit Messengers, the Gans, to enlighten them, but they would not listen. Distressed by such ignorance, the Gans decided to leave, and when The People found only pictures of the Gans at the entrance to their sacred cave, they were overwhelmed with shame. They knew the Gans had returned to a place untarnished by human hands and, after much deliberation, The People decided to imitate the Gans to fulfil Usen's Chosen Lifeway. From that moment of understanding on the holy mountain, Dzil Nchaa Si An, what has united the six independent N'dé divisions; The Western, Chiricahua, Mescalero, Jicarilla, Lipan and Kiowa-Apache; the respective sub-divisions, clans and family clusters; is undertaking everyday as a sacred path to be walked in harmony with all creation.

The Sunrise, or Coming Out ceremony, remains the focus of The People's spiritual identity, when a pubescent girl receives power from, and brings life to, Changing Woman. The Gans appear in the Sunrise Ceremony and, looking up to the peak of Dzil Nchaa Si An, their presence comes raining down in the shadows of men, or in spirits dancing from those shadows when flesh and blood has

Pronghorn Antelope

faded and gone. And how they whirl and skip and soar to the heartbeat pounding in the drum, in their chests and through all life. Bringing alive the butterfly whose flight on open wings crowns hoods shrouded by mystery with headdresses splayed like fans of horns that proclaim the Gans to be guardians of those on two legs, and four. Gull and turkey, eagle feathers fly, appealing to the waters, the mountains and Usen's sky, as tongues from voice and flame lap at the darkness, casting a glow on bodies dizzy beneath charcoal, paint and clay. A shower of white dots blur as hail for the pure heart, and smeared in lightning arrows, moons and stars, gleams everlasting light. And God, I know he's coming, encircled in the Power of the sun and daubed red on the cross of the winds and four cardinal directions.

Through it all they return, always whirling and skipping and soaring to the heartbeat, curing the sick and healing pain, but soon they may have to dance around a telescope bearing Christopher Columbus' name. In the death throes of its Second Session, the 104th Congress received 'Amendment No. 173', a rider withdrawing funds from '. . . the Indian Health Service to prepare a report on HIV-AIDS prevention', in favour of constructing a third telescope on 'Mount Graham'. Looking south from the San Carlos Apache reservation, Dzil Nchaa Si An protrudes above the Pinaleno Mountains, an incentive if one were needed for The People to continue their protests. What use is looking into the heart of the universe if you are blind to the heart on earth?

'You might see all them, you know, who became clan leaders, down there where Cochise and the others hung out', a young San Carlos woman suggested, with her daughter wrapped around her leg, hinting with a tug that she wanted a pop from the cooler. She didn't look old enough to have a child but when she spoke she was a mother with pride in her little girl, pride in herself and

Gray Wolf

With His brother the wolf, Coyote created the world.

After death, the human spirit then enters the Land of Coyote,

where the wolf revives and bathes the soul,

so it may take its place in eternal peace.

The Final Journey – Western Shoshone

pride in her people. If I never found anything else, that evening I found hope for the future. Sliding a finger across the map, Chiricahua National Monument is squeezed between the Dos Cabezas, Dragoon, Swisshelm and Pedregosa 'Sky Islands'. But scale on paper is an acquaintance, not a friend. When the sun finally consented and coaxed the night away, tepid

White-tailed Deer

rays washed over the boney figures emerging for morning prayers. Standing in their eternal temple, like emaciated monks worshipping Buddha and replicas of Buddha all poised in meditation, the eroded rhyolite-tuff contours of Chiricahua National Monument watch and wait. The Chiricahua Apaches describe the area as 'The Land of Standing Up Rocks'. Within the rocks and the smudges of oak and pine, The People's clan custodians, the eagle, butterfly, roadrunner and bear, watch but will not wait.

The butterflies spoilt me, Weidemeyer's admirals and California sisters applauding the air in tiny clouds, one drifting pied, the second ablaze. I put the roadrunner's absence down to a busy Sonoran schedule and, although he hadn't shown, the bear and I usually manage to talk. These are not days for disappointments, or 'what might have been'. A white-tailed fawn busily browsing didn't relish my company, and let me know with a display of impudent feigned butts before his mother appeared and stamped, caught in two minds between a cough and a sneeze – the sound of the white-tails' warning. Watching them spring away in their perfectly tailored greyish-tan and cinnamon coats with white plumed tails raised and flared, I can see why only the Gray One, the clown among the Gans, would choose to ride a deer instead of a horse. 'Itza-chu, Itza-chu'. Faint yet harsh, far in the distance, the eagle circled, calling its 'Apache' name. For those who don't believe, the eagle calls to them to watch and welcome the tangible, the emissary of the Creator, gliding from the known, to behind,

and the other world, with the thoughts of the believers raised high and carried on the wing to the warmth of the sun. The eagle's soul, passed on through its feathers, offers sacred healing and spiritual influence. Among The People, a feather represents a prayer to banish 'enemies against Power'. In battle, each feather worn with pride on the Plains honours the spirit of a fallen warrior. Although cast on the four winds, across the mountains, deserts and plains, in every heart the eagle's sanctity prevails.

Within the monument's northern boundary, the 'Cochise Head' rock formation wears a stare that is heaven bound. 'The Land of Standing Up Rocks', the Dragoon Mountains and Mexico's Sierra Madre range, were the strongholds of Cochise, and later, Geronimo. Their names, like those of Nana, Victorio, Mangas Coloradas, Juh and Naiche, will never be forgotten, but on the battlesites and throughout the pages of weighted infamy, the terms son, brother, father, husband, uncle and grandfather are omitted. All were Chiricahuas from the Chokonen, Chihinne, Nednhi and Bedonkohe bands. And all were men with families. Under the scrutiny of Santa Fe's idols and infidels, Mangas Coloradas signed a treaty in 1852 to protect the Chiricahuas from the descending bullets, sabers, cannon balls and ropes. But then gold and silver and Apache hair was discovered. In Chihuahua and Sonora, a man's scalp sold for 100 pesos, a woman's brought 50 pesos and a child's worth was placed at 25 pesos. North of the border, the bounty rose to $250 per Apache scalp. Prospectors, murderers and slave traders got rich on Manifest Destiny in the southwest. Dead or alive, an Apache had a price.

When their loved ones perished, they fought. And when they were robbed and starving, they raided. With every violation against them, their resistance became more dogged and their vow to avenge set ruthless. 'It is better to die fighting than to starve', insisted Victorio, as he saw 'babies almost devoured by insects' in the squalid confines of the old San Carlos agency. 'Men do things in war they do not do in peace', Cochise reminded General Oliver O. Howard, when the President's peace envoy eyed an army rifle in the hands of a Chokonen man. If Howard had been inclined to remember, Cochise's words would have appeased his contrition as two US army officers, Captain Edmond Shirland and General Joseph West, were responsible for the murder of Cochise's father-in-law, Mangas Coloradas.

Shirland deceived Mangas with peaceful overtures. Initially, Mangas was suspicious, he'd reached for the American's hand in friendship before at the Santa Rita copper mines in 1837 when his people were welcomed to a fiesta then massacred as they ate. And the scars on his back reminded him of his last attempt to parley, when the folks of Pino Altos rewarded his efforts by binding him to a tree for bullwhipping. But when Shirland posted a white flag, Mangas tried again. 'I want him dead or alive in the morning. Do you understand, *I want him dead*', General West informed the camp guards, who proceeded to torture the prostrate seventy-year-old Chihinne leader by applying red hot bayonets to the soles of his feet and legs. When Mangas protested, they shot and scalped him, before decapitating his body and boiling the flesh from the skull, which was hastily sold to a phrenologist.

In 1872 Cochise and Howard reached an agreement and Tom 'Chickasaw' Jeffords, the only white-American to genuinely know Cochise, was appointed Indian Agent for the Chiricahuas. The peace, and Howard's word, lasted until Cochise's death in 1874 during the Season When The Leaves Are Dark Green. 'He was a man who scorned a liar', said Jeffords of Cochise, 'his religion was truth and loyalty'.

And then there was Goyahkla. 'I did not pray, nor did I resolve to do anything in particular for I had no purpose left', he recollected, choking on how love lay bleeding.

Prairie Dog

His wife, Alope, and their three children, had been his life until the sight of their mutilated bodies tossed beside that of his mother, shattered his reason for being. Sonoran army divisions had marched on the village at Kas-Ki-Yeh, secure in the knowledge that the warriors were trading in Janos. The next time troops from Arispe confronted Chiricahuas they faced those absent men, and in a battle that raged for two hours, the Mexicans pleaded for one of their saints to save them. 'Geronimo' they screamed before dying, and those who escaped gave the name to the warrior whose ferocity they recounted with fear.

Envied, respected, adored or despised, tragedy was the only constant in Goyahkla's life. He married Nana-tha-th-tith and fathered her child but both mother and infant were taken from him in a blizzard of sabers and bullets. When the fury struck Shegha, Goyahkla's third wife and a member of Cochise's family, The Power he had found in grief, and his will that The People survive, *or die*, as Usen intended, inspired his bitter struggle that ended with a third of the US Army pursuing him and twenty-four fighting men. Goyahkla and his small band of starving people surrendered to General Nelson Miles in Skeleton Canyon, Arizona, on 4 September 1886, after Lt Charles B. Gatewood had located their camp in the Sierra Madres and informed them that all of the Chiricahuas, including their families, had been sentenced to confinement in Florida. Miles' terms were two years' imprisonment in Florida, after which Goyahkla and his followers would be relocated to a reservation in Arizona. Goyahkla accepted Miles' promise and died a prisoner of war in February 1909 at Ft Sill, Oklahoma, the closest he ever came to returning to Arizona. The Chiricahuas are still waiting for a reservation in their name.

In 'The Land of Standing Up Rocks', some people only hear echoes dying in the silence of empty canyons, but others say that here the wind still carries his name and so I listen for it calling 'Goyahkla'.

Itza-chu

'I was born upon the prairie,

where the wind blew free and there was nothing to break the light of the sun.

I was born where there were no enclosures and where everything drew a free breath . . .

I lived like my fathers before me, and like them, I lived happily.'

Ten Bears – Comanche

Ambrose, Stephen E., *Crazy Horse and Custer* (Meridian, 1975).
Bear, Luther Standing, *Land Of The Spotted Eagle* (Houghton Mifflin, 1933).
Brown, Dee, *Wondrous Times On The Frontier* (Arrow, 1994).
Brown, Dee, *Bury My Heart At Wounded Knee* (Holt Rineheart and Winston, 1970).
Carroll, John M., *The Benteen – Goldin Letters* (University Of Nebraska Press, 1991).
Connell, Evan S., *Son Of The Morning Star* (Picador, 1986).
Courlander, Harold, *The Fourth World Of The Hopis* (University Of New Mexico Press, 1987).
Deloria Jr, Vine, *Custer Died For Your Sins* (University Of Oklahoma Press, 1988).
Geronimo, *His Own Story* (E. P. Dutton and Co., 1970).
Goodman, Ronald, *Lakota Star Knowledge* (Sinte Gleska University, 1992).
Hauptman, Laurence M., *Between Two Fires* (Free Press, 1995).
Josephy, Alvin M., *The Nez Perce Indians* (University Of Nebraska, 1979).
Josephy, Alvin M., *500 Nations* (Hutchinson/Pimlico, 1995).
Kammen, R./Lefthand, J./Marshall, J., *Soldiers Falling Into Camp* (Affiliated Writers Of America Inc., 1992).
Kaywaykla, James/Ball, Eve, *In The Days Of Victorio* (University Of Arizona Press, 1970).
Kluckholm, Clyde/Leighton, Dorothea, *The Navajo* (Harvard University Press, 1974).
Mails, Thomas E., *The People Called Apache* (BDD, 1974).
De Mallie, Raymond J./Parks, Douglas R., *Sioux Indian Religion* (University Of Oklahoma Press, 1987).
De Mallie, Raymond J., *The Sixth Grandfather: Black Elk's Teachings, Given To John G. Neihardt* (University Of Nebraska Press, 1984).
Mech, L. David, *The Way Of The Wolf* (Voyageur Press, 1991).

BIBLIOGRAPHY & RECOMMENDED READING

Momaday, N. Scott, *The Way To Rainy Mountain* (University Of New Mexico Press, 1969).
Neihardt, John G., *Black Elk Speaks* (W. Morrow and Co., 1932, University Of Nebraska Press, 1988).
Parker, Kathleene, *The Only True People* (Thunder Mesa, 1991).
Petersen, D./Carey, A. D., *Among The Elk* (Northland, 1988).
Rice, Julian, *Black Elk's Story* (University Of New Mexico, 1991).
Sandoz, Mari, *Crazy Horse* (University Of Nebraska Press, 1961).
Schlesier, Karl H., *The Wolves Of Heaven* (University Of Oklahoma Press, 1987).
Smith, P. David, *Ouray* (Wayfinder Press,1986).
Spence, Lewis, *North American Mythology* (Studio Editions, 1993).
Thom, Laine, *Becoming Brave* (Chronicle, 1992).
Timber, John Stands In/Liberty, Margot, *Cheyenne Memories* (University Of Nebraska Press, 1972).
Turner, Frederick, *North American Indian Reader* (Penguin, 1977).
Utley, Robert M., *The Lance And The Shield* (Henry Holt, 1993).
Utter, Jack, *American Indians* (National Woodlands, 1993).
Walker, James R., *Lakota Belief and Ritual* (University Of Nebraska Press, 1991).
Westhorp, C./Collins, R., *Guide To Native Americans* (Salamander, 1993).
Woolworth, Anderson, *Through Dakota Eyes* (Minnesota Historical Press, 1988).

The Trail Of Many Spirits is Serle Chapman's first book. Published in the UK on October 24, 1996, the first printing of *The Trail Of Many Spirits* sold out in under twelve weeks. His writing background stems from freelance journalism and magazine editing. In 1994 he won two national design and marketing awards for Further Education publications. His photography is displayed at the Las Vegas Natural History Museum and in exhibitions across the USA. One of Europe's leading photography magazines, *Amateur Photographer*, included *The Trail Of Many Spirits* within its 1996 'Books of the Year'.